Getting on With Your Children

by

Carol Baker

Illustrated by

Bill Piggins

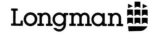

Longman Group UK Limited
Longman House
Burnt Mill, Harlow, Essex CM20 2JE, England
and Associated Companies throughout the World

© Carol Baker 1990

First published 1990

British Library Cataloguing in Publication Data
Baker, Carol, 1944–
    Getting on with your children. – (Successful parenting
    guides).
    1. Children. Interpersonal relationships with parents
    I. Title   II. Series
    306.874

    ISBN 0-582-050340

Set in 10/11 Gill Sans

Produced by Longman Group (FE) Ltd.

Printed in Hong Kong

Contents

Becoming a parent

Being a parent

Every parent-child relationship hits bumpy patches from time to time. Perhaps our children behave in ways we don't like – they may seem argumentative, disobedient and uncooperative. Or WE behave in ways we don't like – perhaps we are short tempered, bored, worried. We sense our relationship isn't as warm and constructive as we'd like but we don't quite know how to change it.

Often our relationship is in a rut. We keep repeating the same old problems, dealing with difficulties in the same way and we seem to be making no headway. This is when we need to stand back, take a long hard look at what's happening and be more creative about tackling our problems.

In the process we can come to enjoy and appreciate our children more and to feel happier about ourselves as parents. As a first step to understanding we have to look carefully at ourselves and our children to see how our past and personalities affect our relationship.

The best and the worst

Parenthood is full of surprises and contradictions. It bring out the best in us. It brings out the worst. We find new depths of tenderness, love and selflessness we never even dreamed we were capable of. We also experience rage, frustration and disappointment at a new level of intensity. We hadn't bargained for these emotions. We may feel shocked, disappointed, confused by our own feelings. We may at times worry we are a failure or a 'bad' parent because we fall short of our high ideals. Or we feel our child is a failure because they don't seem to live up to our expectations.

At a workshop I ran for parents we listed the feelings – the good the bad and the ugly – that we all experience as parents. Our combined list included:

overwhelming love and affection	
hope	belonging
warmth	despair
pride	anger/rage
powerlessness	shame
sadness	uncertainty
frustration	boredom
anxiety	pity
embarrassment	guilt
jealousy	worry

Interestingly, it was the warm or 'good' feelings that people admitted to first. Only gradually, and with some embarrassment, did parents begin to own up to the difficult or 'bad' feelings. But each 'confession' was greeted with recognition – we'd all been there and there was a sense of relief to know we all shared feelings of guilt and failure. The difficulties of being a parent, as well as the pleasures, are common to us all.

If children were able to articulate their feelings perhaps their list would be the same as the adults'.

The myth of the perfect parent

Although rationally we know life isn't perfect and neither our children nor ourselves can be perfect, somewhere at the back of our minds lurks an idealised standard against which we often measure ourselves and feel a failure. We may sometimes meet people who seem to be perfect parents or who seem to have perfect children. So when we lose our cool, or feel mind-blowingly bored and our children whinge and bicker, we imagine other people manage these problems a whole lot better. This makes us feel more inadequate and guilty.

The 'good enough mother'

The child psychiatrist Dr. Winnicott coined the phrase the 'good enough mother' to release us from the tyranny of the myth of the perfect parent. What children need are parents who can keep them safe and who can be sufficiently in tune with them to meet enough of their emotional needs. This will allow the child to grow up trusting that the world is a reasonably good place to be, to feel they are loved and cared for, to be able to love others in return and to develop as both an individual and a social being.

There is of course an underlying paradox in the idea of a perfect parent. Even if such a parent existed who could meet their child's every need and always be unfailingly patient, such a parent would provide a totally unrealistic preparation for life.

Within the relatively safe boundaries of the family, children hopefully experience the good things like care, love, trust, acceptance. But they must also be exposed to the difficult things like anger, loneliness, frustration. The 'good enough parent' doesn't protect their child from all these experiences but tries to order family life in such a way that the child has to deal with the painful feelings in relatively small doses and against a general background of love and support. The 'good enough parent' stands alongside their child and offers support and help in coming to terms with life's difficulties.

Our own childhood

We all have certain memories of our own childhood. These are tantalising windows which provide fleeting glimpses into a past world. But however good our recall we can only account for a minute fraction of the day-in day-out events and feelings that are now lost to our conscious mind for ever. Nonetheless we still carry our inner child within us and we experience moments – particularly when we are strongly aroused – when we are closely in touch with that child. Powerful feelings such as anger, frustration, loneliness can sometimes hit us with an intensity which may not be justified by the actual situation. This is often because we have triggered very early feelings that relate to our own childhood.

Our inner child is both a potential help and a potential hindrance when it comes to bringing up our own children. It's our inner child who enjoys clowning around, being silly and having fun with our children. In addition it's our inner child who can help us understand how it feels to be small and helpless. So that when, for example, our toddler is terrified when he comes eyeball to eyeball with the neighbour's dog we can identify with that fear or draw upon some similar memory of being frightened to help us relate to our child's anxiety.

But our childhood feelings must be filtered through a more adult perspective if we are to use them to understand and help our children. Otherwise we too would stand transfixed with panic or be overwhelmed with anger or loneliness. What we can offer our children is both the understanding of how it feels to be a child and the adult strength and authority to support them emotionally and physically.

Empathy

The instinctive ability to put ourselves in our children's shoes, which comes in part from memories of our own childhood and using our imagination sensitively, is empathy. Empathy is one of our most important assets as a parent. It is very different to sympathy which is feeling sorry **for** our children. Empathy is feeling **with** them.

Empathy enables us to know how our children feel and to respond appropriately. When we are in touch with our children in this way we are tuned in and instinctive in how we behave. For instance when our toddler falls down in the street there are several responses we could make:

- ignore the situation and carry on as if nothing has happened;
- distract their attention perhaps pointing out the postman emptying the letter box;
- use humour – stamping theatrically on the offending pavement to punish it;
- reassure the child everything's all right and there's no harm done;
- comfort the child.

In order to judge how to react we will quickly weigh up several factors including how badly our child has been hurt and their temperament. For instance if we know our child is inclined to make a fuss at the slightest thing we may be fairly brisk and business-like to discourage a scene. But if we see the injury is serious we are more likely to give a hug and sympathy. We will weigh up these various factors so quickly we may not even be aware we have made a decision. We have empathised with the child and instinctively adopted the best course of action.

The unhelpful inner child

We all have emotional black spots: certain experiences or situations which trigger primitive feelings and cause us to over-react when dealing with our own children. However sensible, rational or mature we may be most of the time we will occasionally tune in to our own hurt or angry inner child when something in our present situation triggers off painful past experiences. We won't necessarily make the connection between our past and present nor even realise we are acting unreasonably. But we all do sometimes.

For example a new father may feel resentful and angry towards his baby. He feels distressed and angry at being exluded and shut out from the close relationship he previously enjoyed with his wife. He may not even be able to recognise that the unease which he feels is jealousy. If he does, he may feel shocked – how can he be jealous of his own child? But this situation may have reactivated feelings he had as a child when a sibling was born and he felt displaced from mother's affections and resentful of the intruder. That hurt and jealous child of yesterday can still haunt the grown man of today.

Similarly, a woman who, as a child, experienced a painful separation from her parents – perhaps through a stay in hospital or a divorce – may find it hard to help her children deal with the inevitable separations of growing up. She may over empathise with their anxiety when she has to leave them at playgroup or with a friend. The anxious child within the mother is re-awakened. The mother cannot convey the necessary confidence nor give reassurance to her own children and instead communicates her anxiety to them. Separation becomes a problem for her children and so her past is inappropriately recreated in her children's present.

Most of us have probably shocked ourselves at sometime by responding to our child's temper tantrum or crying by yelling in rage or bursting into tears ourselves. We may feel ashamed afterwards. Where on earth did that raw anger or those tears come from? In all probability it was the despair or frustration of our own inner child that simply couldn't take any more.

Does this mean then that we are all prisoners of the past, bound to re-enact our own past scripts in our children's lives? The answer on the whole is no, though most of us will sometimes re-face and hopefully resolve some of the difficulties from our past when we bring up our children.

Getting help

Any parent who has experienced particularly traumatic events in their childhood which they haven't come to terms with or who finds it very hard to get on with their children might help themselves and their children by seeking some professional counselling help. We cannot change our past but some of the damage can be healed.

Memories of our own parents

Like it or not, the way we bring up our children is coloured by the way our parents brought us up. Some of their attitudes and behaviours we will choose to adopt consciously. Others we may definitely want to change but there will be times when we catch ourselves sounding or behaving just like our own parents. The past can still catch us unawares.

Our children also give us an opportunity to re-write our life script and make good some of the things that went wrong or seemed to be missing in our own childhood. If, for instance, our parents gave us little attention we may have strong feelings about being more involved and available for our own children. Or, if our parents were always harsh and critical we may want to be more positive and supportive to our own children. Parenthood can be a healing element in our lives when we can succeed in breaking those patterns that seemed negative and destructive in our own lives. We are richer for enjoying again some of the good things from our own past and giving to our children some of the things that were missing for us.

But in trying to right earlier wrongs there is always a danger that we topple too much in the opposite direction. If, for example, we had parents who were very authoritarian and strict we may well determine not to put our children through the same regime. If we take this too far we may fail to exert sufficient control over our children.

If, as a result, we surrender our parental discipline our children may in fact end up controlling us. In this way we suffer twice over: we were controlled by our parents and, because we never succeed in getting to grips with our own authority as a parent, we are controlled again by our own children. Our children in their turn miss out on experiencing adults who feel confident and strong enough to impose some limits.

Becoming a parent ourselves also gives us an opportunity to understand our own parents and some of the difficulties they faced. As we become more understanding and forgiving and are united in our common interest in the next generation we may find our relationship with our own parents becomes warmer.

What kind of parent are you?

Most of us develop a style of parenting which evolves from our own personality and attitudes as well as our own family experiences. Researches have defined four main categories of parenting styles. We probably recognise bits of ourselves in each category but may find one description fits our general pattern of parenting more closely than the others.

1 Overprotective parents

The overprotective parent has a very close relationship with their child. In fact the parent-child relationship can sometimes compensate for a lack of closeness between the two parents. The overprotective parent tends to fight the child's battles and baby the child long after she is well able to do things for herself.

Children of over protective parents may be passive, dependent and lack initiative. They lack self-confidence, partly as a result of never having had opportunity to test out their own skills and independence, and partly because they are constantly receiving messages about their inability to cope. Such children often feel anxious and doubt their own competence.

2 Permissive parents

In a family where there is coldness or no affection, permissiveness may indicate a parent who is indifferent or uncaring about their child. Permissiveness in a warm and loving family can mean children are over-indulged and spoiled. Permissive parents don't believe in imposing restraints on their children's behaviour. For instance, they may not expect them to fall in with family routines such as mealtimes and bedtimes.

Children reared in this way may find it difficult consequently to fit in with the expectations of society. They may be aggressive, have difficulty sharing and taking turns. They tend to run wild and have to learn to moderate their behaviour if they are not to become very unpopular with other people.

The positive side of children who are reared by permissive parents is they tend to be confident, independent and creative.

3 Authoritarian parents

These parents lay down the law and expect total obedience from their children. They are nor prepared to negotiate, explain their reasons nor make allowances. They often use physical punishment to discipline their children or frighten them with outside discipline such as calling a policeman.

The children of authoritarian parents are often motivated by fear. They behave well only when they are under threat and consequently fail to develop such qualities as honesty, helpfulness, or consideration for others. If physical coercion has been a major means of control in their life, they are also likely to be aggressive themselves.

4 Authoritative parents

Authoritative parents will set fairly clear guidelines on such matters as bedtimes, mealtimes and acceptable behaviour. However they have a very different way of enforcing rules compared with the authoritarian parent. Authoritative parents explain reasons for rules and encourage children to take responsibility for their own decisions and actions. Although they have a warm relationship with their children they encourage them to be appropriately independent. They are sufficiently flexible to allow the child to have a reasonable say in family decisions but they are always ultimately in charge.

Research suggests that this style of parenting produces children who are well-behaved and self-reliant with a high self-esteem and a sense of right and wrong. They are seldom aggressive and tend to be popular with other people. On the negative side, authoritative parents sometime produce children who are too conforming and well-behaved for their own good.

Our children's personality

Of course it's not only **our** personalities that determine the kind of parent we are or the kind of person our child becomes. Our children are the other half of the child-parent relationship and their personality and the feedback they give us affects both how they develop as well as how we respond to them. There is a constant and changing two way reaction between us and them. Our children shape us as much as we shape them.

It's often not until we have our second child that we fully recognise the individual personality of each of our children. Suddenly we have a point of comparison, a measure. With our first child we tend to assume a high degree of responsibility for everything that goes right and everything that goes wrong. But second and later children help us to realise each child comes into the world with their own individual temperament. We notice for example, that one child may be difficult to handle while their sibling is comparatively easy going. One is more tense or fractious while the other is more relaxed and laid back. Or perhaps one child is fearless and loves new challenges while the other is easily alarmed and anxious.

Some differences of course can be explained by the fact that **we** develop and change with each subsequent child. It's probably true that most parents are more uptight and anxious with first children and more relaxed and permissive with later children. And the circumstances in which we live can be different with each child. But there are still many differences which can only be explained in terms of the child's innate personality. This can be noticed even before birth when one child may be much more active than another in the womb.

Some children seem to be comparatively 'easy' from the beginning. They soon get into a routine and sleep and feed easily. They are friendly, outgoing, with a sociable disposition. Other children may seem to be 'difficult' from the beginning. They are irregular in their feeding and sleeping patterns. They may be excitable or easily upset and withdawn. These children need careful and consistent handling but with patience they can learn to get on with others. Other children may fall into a 'slow to warm up' category. They cannot be rushed into new situations. They are initially timid and anxious but, given time and encouragement, come out of their shell and gain confidence.

Other influences

Character traits are not unchangeable and environment and handling can modify a child's

initial temperament. Clearly some forms of parental handling are going to be more effective or detrimental with certain children than with others. For example the 'slow to warm up child' with over protective parents may well receive the sympathetic handling that he needs. But he is unlikely to get the encouragement and opportunity to try new experiences. If, for example, when he shows his dislike of new food his parents remove it from his diet or if, when he reacts against starting playgroup his parents keep him at home, then he is never helped beyond the stage of initial refusal. Consequently, his life can be seriously limited.

and temper tantrums to find our previously outgoing child suddenly becomes clingy and doesn't want to leave us. By the time we've got them through that stage and gently eased them into playgroup we find they're getting bored at home and wanting constant entertaining and trips to friends. We settle them into school and things may calm down for a while. Then we hit adolescence. Our child becomes moody or defiant. They contradict us and struggle against any restraints we try to impose, but the positive side of change is the fascination and pleasure of watching and helping our children in their move towards independence and growth.

Ages and stages

Our children are constantly developing and changing. Consequently our role as parents is always shifting. Sometimes it seems no sooner have we learned to deal with one set of problems than we're having to pick our way through a whole new lot. We come through the baby problems of colicky evening crying

A mixed bag

One way and another there are an enormous range of influences that come together and affect the way we get on with our children. It is helpful if we can understand these. In this way we can draw upon our strengths and compensate for weaknesses and be more tolerant towards ourselves and our children for those things we find particularly difficult.

Helping your child to feel good

Winning ways with your child

When children feel loved and good about themselves they are more likely to behave in a good and loving way. When they feel competent and capable they become increasingly competent and capable. When they feel trusted they become trustworthy. In other words, treating our children in a positive way makes them behave positively.

The most important gift we can bestow on our children is to love them, think the best of them and believe they are essentially good. For if we don't believe in them who else will? Parents are vitally important in influencing a child's view of themselves. We hold up a mirror for them. When we believe they are intrinsically good and loving then they absorb and internalise this view of themselves. Moreover,

when a child's early experiences make them feel welcomed and good then they continue to believe the world is on the whole a friendly and welcoming place.

Developing our children's self esteem doesn't make them selfish or self-centred as some people might fear – quite the reverse. Liking oneself and holding oneself in esteem is the beginning of loving and respecting other people.

The destructive power of criticism

If, on the other hand, we are constantly disapproving and critical of our children, always seeing the worst in them, we reflect back to them a negative view of themselves. The child comes to feel unloved and unloveable and worthless. They experience the world as a hostile and critical place where they can only expect to receive disapproval. They are less able to respond warmly and positively to other people and they treat others with the same lack of care and respect that has been shown to them.

We demonstrate our love and care in many ways. When children feel our positive regard and affection they feel good about themselves and they feel good about us. We get on well together.

If your child's sense of self-esteem appears to need bolstering or if the relationship between you could be warmer or closer then consider whether you could give more positive attention to your child in any of the following ways.

Keep in touch

Touch is one of the most basic forms of assurance one person can give to another. Babies require handling and touching in order to thrive. But even as children grow up, touch continues to give warmth, comfort and reassurance throughout their lives. A lot of tensions and conflicts can be lessened and healed by touching and holding. When we put our arms around a child of any age we communicate together in a way that short circuits the need for words and explanations.

A good antidote to tense and fractious days with a toddler can be to give a massage, perhaps with hand cream after bath time. The physical contact soothes away the irritabilities of the day and literally put us in touch again.

It's often surprising how an angry or tense child can be soothed – all their tension dissipated – by a loving hug, an arm on their shoulder or gently stroking their hair. This can be a far more effective antidote to stress and upset than words. It can create a trusting and loving mood in which feelings can then be expressed and understood.

The power of praise

Many parents seem uncomfortable about praising their children. They fear praise or compliments will make them conceited or complacent. But appropriate praise provides vital encouragement and recognition. It tells children we value them and we value what they do and confirms they're on the right tracks. Praise gives them the necessary encouragement to become even more praiseworthy.

Even as adults we like our partner, friends or colleagues to notice and comment when we do something well – whether we've grown a thriving pot plant, made a speech, experimented with a new meal or produced an interesting piece of work. Recognition and appreciation give us positive feedback and motivates us to strive next time.

And yet it's amazing how often parents criticise, find fault, point out omissions without ever noticing all the many positive things children do. For instance it's easy to be cross and criticise when a child doesn't put their things away, but do we ever notice and comment favourably when they do remember. We may tell our child off for being rude but do

we think to comment when they show consideration and friendliness. Of course we should use praise thoughtfully. Children quickly see through glib flattery. It devalues them and us.

Some useful guidelines for praising children are:

- Be specific when you praise your child. Single out the key aspect of their achievement. When praise is too general or exaggerated the child feels uncomfortable. She knows her work or behaviour can't really be "wonderful . . . terrific . . . amazing" but if you tell her "I get a real sense of movement from your painting," or "that blue sky really makes me think of summer" you indicate a more genuine appreciation. Similarly if you praise her social achievements, "That was very thoughtful of you to make grandma a Get Well card" or "You were very brave when the nurse gave you that injection" we give helpful feedback. The child feels genuinely valued and has clearer guidelines on how to carry on being thoughtful and brave – or whatever the quality is we're praising.

- Never mix praise with criticism. Some parents are so anxious about praising their children they seem almost compelled to add a sting in the tail.

    "Thank you for washing up . . . about time too."
    "You did well to get your spellings all right. Wonders will never cease."

    Barbed praise achieves no positive end. The child hears only the criticism and feels frustrated and hurt that you even use their genuine efforts as an excuse for showing disapproval.

- Don't use praise as a kind of pressure or emotional blackmail. For instance, a child who is constantly told, "You're so good at maths/football you're bound to get a grade A/into the team" will feel under pressure from such high expectations.

- Praise a wide range of achievements. It's worth noting the qualities or behaviours we normally praise. For instance if we only praise a child for compliant behaviour, being good and doing as they're told we may need to introduce more balance by also praising initiative and self-reliance. Similarly, if we find we only praise our child for reading well, getting good marks in their spelling test or having a good end of term report then maybe we should aim to foster greater roundedness by commenting when they draw an interesting picture, think up a clever solution to an everyday problem or show thoughtfulness to their friends.

- Help your child to praise themselves and value their own achievements. Satisfaction must come from within as well as outside the self. Give permission to your child to feel pleased with their achievements.

  "You must feel very proud that you've managed to make that all on your own."
  "If I were you I'd give myself a pat on the back for standing up to a bully like that."

- A very effective means of praising children, particularly those who become embarrassed is to use a technique known as 'earshotting'. This is praising our child to another person but when the child can 'overhear'. Thus if your child 'overhears' you telling your partner or a friend how helpful or grown up they've been this often carries more weight than telling the child directly yourself.

- It's also helpful to our children if we let them see us praising ourselves when we do something we're proud of. When we congratulate ourselves for completing a difficult piece of work, turning out a well risen cake, asserting ourselves with a difficult official then they learn how to give praise to themselves.

Give time and attention

There are probably few of us who feel we give our children as much time as we'd like. The pressure of working outside and inside the home, of dealing with the demands of other people and trying to meet our own needs means we never have as much energy and time for everything as we want. If this problem feels very desperate then maybe we have to rethink priorities. It is possible to get by with less elaborate meals, leave some of the work until after the children are in bed and accept some lower standards.

Whatever the pressures, we do need to give children special time just for them every day. The more children there are in the family the more difficult this becomes. The younger the child the more individual time they need with us and their other care-givers. Being with a child a lot of the time doesn't necessarily guarantee that they get our attention. It is quite possible to spend a whole day alongside a child without ever giving them full attention.

Check there are regular opportunities for real closeness when you can 'tune in' to your child and they know they have your undivided attention. For pre-schoolers at home it might be elevenses or after lunch when you both sit down together to look at a book, play, chat – or just enjoy a quiet cuddle. With school children you may have time to talk and listen on the way to school, when they come home in the evening or at bath or bed time. Help to protect this time from intrusion and show you value your time together by reducing distractions. For instance turn off the boiling potatoes and take the phone off the hook.

Respect your child's privacy

It may seem strange to think of children needing privacy but we all need personal space. Even small babies need time to be alone at times and just contemplate their toes. As they grow older, children need the opportunity to play make-believe games without adult intrusion or comment, store their treasures, have secrets with their friends, experiment with their appearance and simply be on their own.

The trouble is, families can be too much on top of each other and unless we are prepared to draw back and give our children physical and emotional space they can grow up with a sense of being always observed, monitored and called to give account of themselves. They don't have the opportunity to develop their own inner world and reality.

The parent who wants to see all, know all and comment upon everything can be experienced as very intrusive by their child. The only way the child can protect their inner life is to become secretive or withdrawn. At some time we've all asked our child what they did at school or at a friend's house only to get the answer "Nothing much." This tells us the child isn't ready or willing to share their experiences with us – or at least not yet. They have their own world apart from us and it's healthy that we allow them this separateness.

Knowing when to withdraw from a child's life and allow them privacy is a matter of sensitive timing. Privacy is something children seek as they become older and more independent. But even young children may often want to keep something 'secret' and hidden from us. The best course of action is probably to discreetly reassure ourselves that everything is alright and then keep out.

Children often have a strong sense of the integrity of their own body which we need to respect. If they clearly don't want to be tickled or to be passed around to be kissed and cuddled by doting relatives then we must protect them from such intrusions.

The following actions demonstrate to our children that we respect their rights as an individual but they only become appropriate at certain stages in our child's life:

- not 'hearing' or commenting on their make-believe play;
  Children need to fantasise and pretend. They talk to non-existent characters and

take roles in their own fantasy inventions. We should not intrude in this private world nor comment or laugh at their pretend games.

- not embarrassing them in front of other people by recounting their failings or personal foibles;
- not making belittling remarks about their appearance or choice of clothes. People sometimes make the sort of remarks to children they would consider offensive if addressed to themselves or another adult;
- asking before we enter their room;
- not reading their letters, diary or listening into their phone calls;
- not entering the bathroom if they indicate they want to be alone;
- not quizzing them about their friends or activities if they've made it clear they don't want to talk;
- not going through their drawers or cupboards.

As we respect our growing child's privacy the other side of the coin is that we can begin to claim our own rights to more privacy. For instance we may expect our child not to pick up the extension when we're on the phone nor go through our handbag. This is part of the two way traffic that acknowledges each of us as an individual with rights to privacy.

Celebrate your child's life

At some time most of us have been into households which seem to exude an almost hostile and rejecting feeling to the children who live there. The children seem to be constantly in the way, intruders, a nuisance. Their presence seems an unwelcome interruption to the smooth running of busy adult lives or an immaculate household. There is often no evidence that children live there (other than the studio portraits neatly arranged on the mantlepiece.)

Welcoming children into our lives means we have to make both physical and emotional

space for them. Children need physical space to play and store their things. They need to make a mess sometimes. This isn't to say we allow them to wreck the place but there should be some time and place when they can play with water, paint, cook, make sticky collages or leave their Lego models half-completed. In addition, a place where children's paintings can be pinned up on display demonstrates that we value their achievements.

Children also need to feel they have emotional space in our lives – that they are wanted, enjoyed – and celebrated. Spending time, talking and listening and considering children's needs when making family decisions indicates to children that they we value them.

Many children love to hear the story of their own birth (minus any gory bits). To know you looked forward to their arrival and to hear how pleased you were to see them is a wonderfully affirming experience and it's a story children always enjoy.

"What did today?"

Young children enjoy – perhaps before they go to sleep – remembering together the things that have happened during the day – what they've done, who they've seen. My children used to ask for these sessions as "Let's talk about What Did Today." We used to piece our memories of the day together always ending with, ". . . and then you said, 'Let's talk about What Did Today.'"

To sit quietly and recall the events gives meaning and significance to the day. Things that may otherwise have been lost and forgotten are recalled and gathered together and the minutia of everyday life – everything from finding a ladybird under a leaf to going to visit Granny – can be re-lived and celebrated.

If you've had some difficult parts of the day where the child was naughty or you were cross it's often worth mentioning these too if you can do so in a way which isn't going to stir up more anger or doesn't seem like blaming. It's healthy for children to realise we can have strong and angry feelings about each other but these pass and the relationship survives intact.

Give choice – within limits

On the whole children have little control over their lives. They cannot choose their parents, where they live, what happens to them, whether or not they go to school. Our ultimate aim in bringing up our children must be to give them the skills, confidence and discrimination to eventually make decisions about their own lives and so become independent adults.

By letting children make some decisions we give them experience in weighing up situations and learning about cause and effect. More importantly we give them a sense of having some control over their lives and we demonstrate our respect for them by showing that their ideas and needs count.

Usually of course we can only offer a choice within certain limits. It's dishonest and a recipe for conflict to appear to give a child a choice and then object to their decision or try and dissuade them from their chosen option.

From quite a young age children can enjoy making decisions within certain clearly defined limits. For instance you might ask your two or three year old whether to have yogourt or banana custard for lunch or whether they want to go to the park or the library, whether they want to wear their jeans or their red skirt. Provided it's a genuine choice and you're happy to accept their decision this gives the child an opportunity to have some say in the running of their own life.

With experience we learn how important it is to lay down ground rules when we are offering a choice. When we tell our son he can wear what he wants we don't of course reckon on him desiring his summer shorts when the snow is thick on the ground. Or when we take our daughter shopping for shoes we might be able to avoid the conflict over pointed toes and sling backs if we anticipate this issue and

previously eliminate them from the range of options before setting out from home.

Becoming independent

As parents we have to be both close to our children and detached from them. We have to be close enough to love them, care for them and instinctively understand and identify their needs. But we also need to be detached enough to allow them to become separate individuals who can eventually lead their own lives, make their own friends and develop their own skills and personalities. Every child has their own destiny and we cannot live our life through our children.

As well as letting children make their own decisions we have to encourage them to act independently where it's appropriate. For the three year old this may mean encouraging them to dress themselves, for the nine year old it may mean expecting them to pack their own lunch and school bag in the morning. Allowing children to do things for themselves means we have to be patient while they are mastering new skills. In the early stages it's usually quicker to do the job ourselves but our children learn nothing if we always take the easy option.

Other people

As well as giving our children confidence to act for themselves it is in our hands to give the encouragement and permission to form attachments to other people such as grandparents, childminders, relatives, friends and teachers. Some parents find it quite threatening when their child is clearly fond of someone else or enjoys staying away from home. But far from feeling threatened we should rejoice in our child's ability to make independent relationships. It's an indication that a child feels very secure and loved at home when they can use that security as a base from which to step outside towards other people.

Don't live your life through your children

Most of us have hopes and dreams for our children. We want them to be happy, to form fulfilling relationships, find satisfaction in their work and develop their talents. We may also want to give them some of the advantages we missed in our lives. For example the parent who feels with the right support and encouragement she or he might have been a musician, a painter or a doctor may hope to see their dreams fulfilled through their children. The trouble is, their children may have quite different talents. If parents are unwilling to accept this, children may be steered into a life which isn't right for them or if they choose to go in a different direction they may feel guilty and unsupported. Only by keeping an open mind, observing our children's needs and listening and talking with them can we help them to become themselves.

Let your child make mistakes

We all make mistakes. We say the wrong thing, misjudge situations or lack the skills to handle them properly. We forget things. We break things. Children, who are less physically capable and who have less experience of life, are bound to make more mistakes. How we respond to their mistakes affects their confidence and their willingness to try new situations and to take risks in the future. We respond to children's mistakes in various ways. We may:

- ignore the mistake;
- be punitive or critical;
- use mistakes as an excuse to prevent the child doing something in the future;
- use mistakes constructively to see what help our child needs to become more competent;
- point out it's all right to make mistakes.

There is a tendency sometimes to fall upon children's mistakes with something approaching glee. A mistake is seen as a vindication of our superiority against the child's inferiority. When our child falls from the climbing frame we say, "I told you not to climb so high." (If we had really anticipated this outcome then perhaps we should have used our authority to stop the child climbing so high or else have helped them to do so safely.)

Or we may use a mistake as an excuse for controlling a child's behaviour in the future. Because they have broken a cup we forbid them to go to the crockery cupboard or because they fought when their friend came to play we use this as an excuse not to let their friends come round in future. These arrangements may suit us very well and the child's mistake becomes a justification for insisting we get our own way. But the child learns nothing except that they are incompetent and we have no faith in them. Deep down they sense we are capitalising on their weakness. They feel resentful and helpless. If we find ourselves harping on about past failings we should consider very carefully whether we aren't in fact using a child's lack of skill to foster a sense of failure and hence limit and control the child.

Our children's mistakes may, of course, indicate that they aren't yet ready to handle certain situations but there are ways of acknowledging this without putting blame on the child or emphasising his inadequacies.

Mistakes can be useful pointers showing us and the child where they need to adjust their behaviour or where we need to offer more help and support. Thus, instead of banning the crockery cupboard or friends, we could ask our child how they could handle the crocks more carefully. Or we could look at what went wrong when their friend came to play and help them work out how to improve things next time.

If we are punitive or vindictive about mistakes our children become fearful of attempting new situations or developing new skills. Every situation involves the risk of failure. If we exaggerate their failures, children lose faith in their ability to face new situations. The only way they can be sure not to put a foot wrong is to stand still. And that's the most depressing failure of all.

Do we sex stereotype our children

The question of sex stereotyping and children usually generates a lot of controversy. On the one hand there are those who believe that all sex differences are socially conditioned and others who believe that differences between boys and girls are totally innate.

Since we can never bring up a child free from social pressures and expectations the matter is largely unproveable either way. The truth probably lies somewhere between the two points of view: there are innate male and female differences but these are probably considerably exaggerated by conditioning.

Research shows, for example, that parents handle male babies and female babies differently. They are more soothing to female babies. They select soft toys and gentler activities for them. Male babies on the other hand are handled more vigorously. They tend to be bounced up and down and given more active toys. Children's behaviour is also interpreted differently depending on whether the child is a boy or a girl. When parents were shown a video of a baby crying in response to a loud noise the parents who thought the baby was female interpreted the crying as fear whereas parents who believed the baby to be male interpreted the crying as anger.

Once children start school there are differences in the way they are treated. Classroom studies show that boys make more noise, take up more space and demand and receive more teacher time than girls. Girls gain approval by being quiet, biddable and hard working but these qualities often mean they miss out on attention.

Teachers, playgroup leaders, relatives, television, story books and in fact everyone with whom our child comes into contact add to their perception of what it means to be male or female. But home life is still a major influence and it's here parents can subtly challenge and question some of the assumptions that the child meets elsewhere.

Of course our children have to live within society and their peer group as well as within the family and we don't want to turn them into freaks and oddities. But if we look at the general social stereotypes of boys and girls we can see how limiting these can be for both sexes. There are whole areas of personality, behaviour and skills which can become closed off and denied to each sex. If we are aware of this we can do something to counteract these pressures and offer our children a wider repertoire of behaviour and range of experiences.

"A real little girl"

Stereotyped assumptions about girls suggest they are biddable, polite, quiet, socially adept and well mannered. They are clean and tidy and want to be pretty. They are less aggressive than boys. They are guileful and manipulative.

A quick look around any toy shop tends to show that although girls and boys may enjoy many unisex toys up to the age of five, once they start school then boys corner the market for construction, technological and computer toys while girls have more passive toys – dolls, domestic toys and makeup. This can affect the way they see themselves and have important repercussions for future career choices.

To counteract some of the sexist pressures on our daughters we can make sure we give permission for a wide range of different behaviours. The following suggestions might help to keep girls' options as open as possible.

- Let your daughter be noisy, active and express her anger and her aggressive feelings (at least to the same degree as you'd allow a boy.)

- Let her enjoy messy play when appropriate.

- Don't just praise her for passive virtues such as being pretty or well-behaved. Praise her for being brave, resourceful, imaginative, active.

- Talk about how women and girls behave in books and on television. How true is this to real life? As well as traditional fairy stories where the heroine's main attribute is usually prettiness read modern stories with more gutsy active female heroines.

- Encourage your daughter to be interested in and think herself capable of activities involving science, maths and technology. Girls are often turned off these important

subjects because they have less hands-on practice and hence less confidence than their brothers. Encourage problem-solving skills. Involve her in practical DIY tasks around the home. Buy construction kits and make things with her.

- Give her a sense of scope and choice in thinking about what she wants to be when she grows up. You can start this very young. When she builds a shoe box house or takes an interest in space suggest she could one day be an architect or an astronaut. Of course, such suggestions are only tongue-in-cheek at this stage but it helps girls to start thinking of themselves as capable people who can select their future from a wide menu of options.

"Every bit a boy"

Stereotyped assumptions about boys make them out to be tough and naturally brave. They don't cry or make a fuss. (This clearly puts a lot of stress on boys and denies their tender side.) Boys are active, messy and untidy. They are good at maths and have an affinity with machinery and technology. They are straighforward, unsubtle and guileless in relationships.

Most boys' toys, certainly for those of school age, assume that boys are mainly interested in aggression and ugliness.

Clearly this is very limiting view and one which doesn't do justice to the full potential of boys. To help counteract these stereotypes for our sons we need to ensure they are encouraged to develop a wide range of behaviour and skills in the following ways.

- Encourage your son to enjoy some quiet activities and games.

- Give boys permission to express their sadness and pain and to cry if they want.

- Encourage boys to show gentleness and kindness towards other people, especially younger children.

- Expect them to do any domestic tasks that you would expect of a girl the same age.

- Teach him ways to get out of difficulties without resolving to force.

Keeping options open

There's always a danger that, in trying to avoid sexist limitations, we end up imposing a different kind of pressure. We may feel we've failed if our girls head for pretty pink frocks when we go shopping, or if they want dolls or if their sole ambition is to be a Mummy. Or we wonder where we've gone wrong when our sons dash around making machine gun noises.

What's important is to offer alternative ways of thinking and behaving so that the options will be there when and if the child is ready to take them up. We all have many aspects to our personalities and the important thing is to allow our children access to the full range of their personality.

Building confidence

The confident child is the one who says "I can" instead of "I can't." Confidence opens doors to new experiences and new people whereas lack of confidence keeps them firmly shut. The child who is confident can:

- mix with other people;
- make their needs known;
- stand up for themselves and resist pressure from the peer group;
- trust that other people will welcome them;
- attempt to tackle new situations;
- get on with living because they are not inhibited by fear.

Of course no one is ever totally confident all the time. Confidence is a matter of degree. We are more confident about some things than

others and more confident with some people than others. Confidence comes from within ourselves, from our accumulated experiences and from the feedback we get from other people and our environment.

How far confidence is innate and how far it is learned is a matter of debate. Certainly some children seem to be naturally more outgoing and confident from a very early age – smiling at strangers and reaching out for new things – while others are guarded or anxious.

We may have to work more carefully at building confidence in some children than others and even then they may not be as outgoing as their friends or other siblings. But if we can help them to reach a stage where they can make friends, and try new experiences, albeit hesitantly, then we can prevent lack of confidence imposing too great a restriction on their lives.

Confidence begins in the early years when the young child grows up in a sympathetic environment where his needs are largely understood and met. If parents are able to provide security and consistency at this time then the child has a sound base from which to spring off later.

How to help a young child develop confidence

- Be reliable. Don't ever slip away and leave your child unexpectedly. If you are going to leave him with a friend or at playgroup give warning of your departure. It's better to have a few tears on parting rather than the child turn round and find you've gone. That can create longlasting anxieties.

- Never threaten to abandon or leave him – in anger or in jest. Abandonment is one of the greatest psychological anxieties a child can experience. It is too powerful and overwhelming a fear to ever be used as a weapon. It is every child's right to know that no matter what they do we are always there for them.

- Stay alongside your child when he attempts new situations. Whether he's starting play-group or getting used to the swimming baths be with him physically and only withdraw gradually as his confidence increases.

- Don't rush him. Children need time to become accustomed to new faces, places and situations. Expose him to new experiences gradually. It often helps not to focus on him too intently when he is meeting a new person. If you engage the other person in conversation for a little while, thus deflecting the full beam of attention from the child, this gives him a chance to observe and acclimatise to the stranger or the situation without pressure to participate immediately.

- Don't expect him to tackle new situations if he has had some major upheaval in his life such as a new baby in the family or a long separation from you. For a time he may just need to go backwards and make sure his base is still secure.

- Never laught at or ridicule his failures.

- Don't make him grow up too fast or accept too much responsibility too soon. This can cause anxiety which will undermine his developing confidence.

How to help your older child

- Don't compare him unfavourably with other people.

- Praise him for the things he can do.

- Let him know other people sometimes feel anxious and frightened too. This is often a revelation to children who assume they are the only people who feel insecure or worried.

- Don't present yourself as over confident and capable all the time. Let your child know you sometimes worry about things but explain how you cope.

- Be kind but firm when you know your child has the ability to cope or when he simply has no choice about doing something. Be honest about the difficulties but infect him with your confidence that he will manage. Lack of confidence is something to be overcome by degrees and should not be allowed to become an excuse for constant avoidance.

- Teach him relaxation techniques. Show him how to breathe deeply and slowly and remind him to use this when he feels himself becoming anxious.

Understanding your child

Listening to our children

Most of us believe we listen to our children. It seems a fairly simple activity. And yet how often do we **really and truly** listen with fully focused attention to what our children are saying – or not quite managing to say. Or if we do try and draw them out over a particular problem, how often do we get nowhere or find one or other of us gets angry or aggrieved and communication breaks down.

Children communicate their feelings all the time with their words, actions and body language. Even silences and lack of actions tell us something about how a child is feeling. Really hearing and responding to our children's innermost feelings is not easy and there are several reasons why we may find it hard to give a child the space and the permission to talk.

Why we don't hear

The main stumbling blocks to communication are:

Lack of time
If we are always rushing or working against the clock we may simply not have time to tune in to our children's needs.

It helps if we can consciously plan some points in our everyday routine where we switch on to each child. It may be at bath time, bed time, the journey to school or a shared meal. Ideally, this time ought to be fairly stress-free, without interruptions, when we can both relax and feel comfortable together.

If there are several children demanding our attention, it's a good idea to organise the day so that each child knows they have some time just for them. In addition it is often helpful to make each child the particular focus of attention for several days or a week at a time. By making a special effort to observe and get close to one child, to notice how they react to situation, to think about how their life is developing and get to understand their pleasures and anxieties. it's possible to compensate for some of the frustrations and limitations of having to share our time.

We are too pre-occupied with our own problems
When we are particularly concerned with the kind of problems we all have to face at times: difficulties with our job, financial problems, ill health in the family, or stress in our marriage then we may simply not have sufficient surplus energy or interest to respond to our children's needs.

There is no easy answer but we may be able to discipline ourselves to confine our worrying or our unhappiness and to consciously put aside our own anxieties for some of the time in order to be more available for our children.

If we are very distracted our children almost certainly sense something is wrong. It can set their mind at rest to give them a simple explanation. Or, if we can't spell out the problem, we can at least let them know they are not the cause of the problem. Children often feel that they are to blame in some obscure way for their parents' unhappiness and it makes sense to spare them the unnecessary anguish of feeling guilty and responsible.

We don't want to hear

For reasons which may often be deeply unconscious we may not want to know about our child's problems. This may be because:

We feel guilty

If we feel responsible for our child's unhappiness or problems this makes us uncomfortable and therefore we want to deny the child's feelings.

We are frightened of hearing the truth

We may have unrealistic hopes and expectations of our children and of our relationship with them, in which case we may try to shut out anything which doesn't agree with our idealised picture of how we want things to be. For example, if we think families should always be close and loving we may find it hard to allow our children to express their anger or resentment with us or their siblings. Or if we want our child to be successful academically we may not be prepared to hear they are unhappy or failing at school.

We may feel the child's unhappiness somehow reflects badly on us. We protect ourselves from a sense of failure by brushing aside the child's true feelings.

Our children don't choose to confide in us

It seems that some children, either because they seem to be naturally withdrawn, or because they have learned it's risky to expose their fears and their feelings, find it hard to talk. Young children of course will lack the skills and vocabulary to express subtle feelings. Yet even if they don't use words to indicate how they feel they will still express a lot through their actions and behaviour.

All children are reluctant to communicate openly at times. It may be they don't under-stand the cause of their own distress. They may not, for example, be able to make the link between a difficult event like their father being away or the arrival of a new baby and their resentment, anger or sadness.

A child may also be unwilling to admit to us, or even to themselves, that they have "bad" feelings. To own up to jealousy, or anger for example seems shameful as well as risky. Children fear they may put themselves beyond the pale of our affections if they allow us to see their negative side. Or they fear we won't understand; that we may be angry, blaming, unsympathetic.

A child who is having difficulty talking to us about their problem needs sensitive handling. We may have to guess at the cause of their problem, and put their feelings into words for them. Perhaps, for example, one child in the family has been ill and required a lot of our attention. It then seems the last straw when their older brother starts being aggressive and difficult. Tired and stressed, we are likely to give him short shrift. However, what his awkward behaviour may be telling us is that he resents the loss of our attention and quite possibly feels jealous of his younger brother. Putting his feelings into words for him and showing we understand and sympathise will often make the difficulty a whole lot more bearable.

Empathic listening

We listen empathically when we really hear and understand the feelings of the other person. We tune in without preconceived opinions, without judgment or criticism to the feelings that are being expressed as well as the feelings that may not be verbalised. Empathic listening requires a particular kind of concentration and a kind of courage. It takes courage to let our child have anxieties and fears without us feeling we must rush in to provide instant solutions. It takes courage to let our child really experience their hurt or anger and to share those feelings with them.

It is extremely difficult to listen and respond sensitively – especially if we were not encouraged to express our own feelings when we were children. It's an art we may have to practise and work at. We can so easily and inadvertently stop the flow of communication. We miss the cues that something is wrong. Or we rush in with the automatic response which has the effect of closing doors rather than opening them.

The following guidelines can help us to really hear our children. If you are used to listening with one ear or if you usually brush your child's anxieties aside – albeit from the kindest of motives – you may be surprised at the difference it makes to your relationship if you can begin to listen empathically.

Listen with undivided attention
If you can't give your attention when your child wants to talk, explain that you want to wait until you can listen properly and ask if it can wait for a short while. However, it's rarely practical to expect young children to wait more than a few minutes – if that. Immediacy is all-important and it's usually better to put aside your own task for the time being.

If you have to postpone the conversation with an older child, don't forget to come back to the matter at the soonest opportunity. If children feel they are being fobbed off they will soon lose the inclination to bring their problems to you.

Show you are listening
This doesn't mean you have to sit eyeball to eyeball – no one wants the third degree, especially if they have something difficult to say. In fact children sometimes find it easier to talk if you are partially engaged in something else like driving the car or washing up. But give reassurance that you are listening.

Give minimal prompts
Encourage your child to go on speaking by giving encouraging but non-commital prompts such as "mmm . . . I wonder how that made you feel . . . that must have been difficult for you . . . what happened next . . . "

Allow silence
On the whole we have a great fear of silence. We seem to have to fill it up with talk or questions. In fact silences allow an opportunity to reflect on what you are hearing and provide space for the child to elaborate and add to their account. If you are in the habit of responding quickly give yourselves a little time to reflect when your child next communicates something difficult to you.

Don't make snap judgments
Avoid making judgmental comments or reacting strongly (unless of course this is appropriate, if for instance, your child is telling you something dreadful) and avoid criticism while children are talking. The following remarks are the sort of thing which we may often say without thinking but which block communication:

> "that was a stupid thing to do . . . what do you expect . . . can't you do anything right."

The child instantly goes on the defensive. Instead of opening up they clam up. The moment of communication is lost and it is hard to regain the child's trust once we throw it away thoughtlessly.

Avoid instant solutions
When we have a problem we all know how off-putting it is to have some know-all rushing in and telling us what we ought to do. Yet we often fall into this trap with our children. We think we can see the instant remedy to a child's problem and we can't resist telling them. For instance, if a child is being worried or teased by someone else at school it may seem natural to tell them, "Keep out of his way then." If they complain they are struggling with maths we might tell them, "You ought to work harder."

Either of these solutions might ultimately be the answer to the problem but if we throw these in at the beginning we have lost the opportunity to really understand the child's feelings and explore the difficulties. Why, for example, is our child being picked on at school and how does that feel for them? Why do they have a negative attitude towards maths and how can this be overcome?

Moreover if **we** come up with the answers this suggests to our children that they are too incompetent to solve their own problems. What's more, because these are **our** solutions the child doesn't have the same vested interest in making them work that they would if **they** had come up with the solution themselves.

Keep calm
When we hear children expressing uncomfortable feelings such as,

"I'm scared . . ."
"No one will play with me . . ."
"You don't love me as much as Tom . . ." it's always tempting to rush in brandishing emotional Band Aid.

Because we want to protect our children and can't bear to think of them suffering we want to soothe and cover up the pain with instant remarks like:

"But there's nothing to be scared of . . ."
"Of course people will play with you, you've got loads of friends . . ."
"What rubbish, you know I love you and Tom the same."

The child may seem momentarily reassured and that will make us feel a whole lot better. We seem to have sent the problem packing but all we've done is cover it up.

In effect we're telling the child not to be ridiculous. We're depriving him of his own inner reality. Brushing children's feelings aside is sometimes an indication of our own inner panic. We are often protecting ourselves when we reject our child's painful feelings. We may suspect the truth of what they are telling us. We realise they may well be frightened at night . . . that perhaps they are lonely . . . and maybe we aren't as patient with them as we are with their brother but we don't want to know this and so we use reassuring comments to block out painful messages.

But when we hurry to banish children's pain before it even sees the light of day, our children realise we cannot deal with their feelings. They receive an unconscious message that "Even Mummy and Daddy can't cope with my feelings

so they must be really bad. I'd better keep them to myself in future." And so anxiety and pain are suppressed – but they don't go away.

Acknowledge the feelings
Our children are best helped if we can recognise and reflect back their feelings to them in a calm way. If we tell them,

"It's not nice when you're scared . . . "
"You must feel lonely if you think other children don't want to play with you . . ."
"I guess you feel angry and hurt if you think we don't love you as much as Tom . . ."

we show acceptance and understanding. To hear their feelings voiced and fed back can be very powerful. The child knows they've been heard, they are not so alone. They also see that although we understand and know how they feel we aren't thrown and we can cope. The feelings aren't unmanageable. Our acceptance gives the child chance to say more about how they feel and explore the situation.

Reality testing
But accepting the child's feelings doesn't mean we have to accept the child's interpretation of reality. We don't necessarily agree that:

- the situation is scary (although we accept the child is scared) . . .
- that other children really don't want to play with him (though we recognise he nonetheless feels lonely) . . .
- or that we love him less than Tom (although we accept he somehow feels unloved or that we are unfair in our treatment).

We must explore with our child why they feel scared . . . what exactly do they mean when they say other children don't play with them. How many children won't play and how often has this happened? And what makes them think we don't love them as much as their brother? After this we can begin to feed some objectivity into the problem and we can look at how they can deal with their feelings about the situation.

Help children work out their own solutions
The most satisfactory solutions are always those

we work out for ourselves – perhaps with the support of another person. By gentle questioning we can help our child to try and understand the nature of the problem and work towards some solutions.

"Why do you find this scary . . . what would make it less frightening?"
"Why do you think other children won't play with you . . . can we try and think of some ways of getting round this?"
"What is it exactly that makes you think I don't love you as much as your brother, I wonder what would make you realise how special you are to me?"

Others feel the same

It's helpful to discuss with children that other people sometimes feel the same as they do. This isn't to take away the uniqueness of their experience but, until they are told, children have no way of realising that at times other people also feel frightened, lonely or unfairly treated. It can be a revelation and very reassuring to know this. You might be able to recall some time when you felt afraid of the dark when you were a child. You can point out

that many children feel no one will play with them sometimes. Ask him to think which other children may be lonely. He may also realise there are times when Tom thinks he's unfairly treated too.

When actions speak louder than words

Of course children don't always express their feelings with words. They are not always clear about what they are feeling, or they are frightened to reveal 'bad' feelings. Often when children are most in need of love and understanding they behave in ways that make them very unloveable. They become their own worst enemies and seem set on making enemies of us.

Children's anti-social behaviour is often their way of giving us an important message. The message may be, "I feel . . . hurt . . . lonely . . . unloved . . . ignored . . . rejected . . . angry . . . life isn't fair." Children have a wide repertoire of

behaviour to express their negative feelings – anything from kicking the table, looking sullen and morose, shouting, silent withdrawal, needling you or their siblings, creating arguments – and many other tactics which will be familiar to you.

We have to make it clear to our children when we won't stand for the behaviour but we can still show we want to understand the hurt or angry feelings underneath. If we choose to ignore the feelings and simply attack their behaviour we often make the situation a lot worse. Not only is the child stuck with their original grievance but they are now in trouble and misunderstood as well. If we refuse to hear what the child is really feeling we compel them to misbehave even more in order to try and get their feelings home to us. Thus they kick the table harder, become doubly sullen, shout even louder and the problem escalates. Only when we acknowledge the underlying emotions can the child let go of the distress which is causing them to behave badly. Thus when our child comes home from school bad tempered and only answering in monosyllables we might feel a bit aggrieved: what have we done to deserve this? Unhelpful responses would be:

"I see you're your usual cheerful self today."
"I refuse to speak to you until you snap out of this."

Rejecting comments compound the child's sense of hurt and isolation. A more helpful response might be:

"I've got the feeling something's gone wrong today. Do you want to tell me about it?"

Similarly, when our adolescent bangs the doors and responds to us with grunts we can either just address the behaviour, "Stop banging the doors!" "Talk to me properly." which will only increase the tension between us. Or we can choose to go to the heart of the problem:

"I've got the feeling you're mad at me because I said you can't go to the disco at the weekend. Am I right?"

This gives your child a chance to get his feelings into the open, to express his disappointment and anger directly instead of attacking you through slamming the doors. Even when we have caused our child's anger, perhaps because we have withheld permission for them to go somewhere, we've asked them to do something they don't want, or we've refused to buy something they want, we can still empathise with their feelings of disappointment. If we can say, "I understand your disappointment and I know how difficult this is for you" the child can take some comfort from knowing we empathise with their loss and our relationship suffers less damage.

Sometimes we can guess at what lies behind their mood. At other times we're in the dark. But even when children don't use words to tell us of their distress we can still use our Empathic Listening techniques.

A comment like, "You seem upset today I wonder what's troubling you," will often help us reach beyond the behaviour and get in touch with the feelings. It's helpful for children to hear their feelings put into words for them. Even an angry or bolshy child will sometimes subside – perhaps into tears – with a loving arm around their shoulder and a message that you understand and care about how they feel.

A summary

We can get a whole lot closer to our children if we are prepared to spend time and effort listening to what they have to say. The steps to empathic listening are:

- make time to listen;
- listen with undivided attention;
- give minimal prompts;
- allow silences;
- don't make snap judgments;
- avoid instant solutions;
- keep calm;
- acknowledge the feelings;
- help the child work out their own solutions.

Difficult feelings: Helping yourself and your child

When you don't like your child

We seldom like to admit it but most of us find there are times when we feel out of tune with our children. Even though we generally get on well with them we can hit difficult patches when we seem to feel out of step with each other. We may be constantly annoyed or frustrated and everything our child does seems to rub us up the wrong way. Our negative feelings in turn make our children more difficult and we are both caught in a vicious circle.

This can be desperately worrying and make us feel guilty. We want to love our child but somehow we just don't seem able to find the loving feelings. Even when we make a real effort things still seem to go wrong.

We can't expect our children to put things right. We are the adults; the ones who must take the initiative to try and shift the relationship into a more positive gear. If you have never felt able to love your child then this is a long term difficulty that might be helped by seeking some counselling or therapy for yourself. But generally you will be able to improve your relationship by adopting some of the suggestions in the second chapter . . . and coming to understand why things may be going wrong.

Underlying difficulties

In trying to tease out the various elements that can underly difficulties in our relationships we should ask ourselves the following questions:

- Is this just a normal phase of my child's development?
- Are my expectations realistic?
- Is my child affected by stress in their life?
- Am I affected by stress in my life?
- Is there some stress within the family or the immediate environment?
- Is there something in my child's personality or previous experience that is causing difficulties?
- Is there something in my personality or previous experience that is causing difficulties?
- Am I handling the situation in the best way. How could I manage things differently?
- Is my child clear about what behaviour I expect?

Let us look in more detail at some of these possible difficulties.

Normal development

Every phase of a child's development requires some new learning and adjustment – by both the child and us. Some phases seem to be more difficult than others. The toddler for instance is developing a strong inner drive to do things for herself and make her own decisions. But she hasn't yet learned to consider other people's needs or postpone gratification of her desires.

So when we frustrate her powerful inner drives by saying No, there is an emotional explosion.

Or the three year old may be very anxious about separations, which can create difficulties when we leave her at playgroup or nursery. This natural phase of development can be exacerbated if the child has an anxious personality (or if we have an anxious personality.) It can be further intensified if there is some stress in the family at the same time, say a new baby, and by inappropriate handling which may be either too unsympathetic or over indulgent.

Ten years later we are likely to be experiencing quite a different problem: the adolescent who is pushing against the limits and for whom the influences of peer behaviour and attitudes are in conflict with the expectations of the family.

One way of determining whether our child's behaviour is normal for their age is to check out with friends who have similar age children. Other parents are a great source of learning and reassurance.

If we feel that on the whole our child's behaviour is fairly typical for their age it's easier to weather the difficulty than if we are worried they are developing into an appalling person or our relationship is breaking down. We know we don't need to panic because the problem is temporary.

However, even when we can accept this as a short term problem we still have to face the problem of how to handle the situation and survive. Empathic listening (page 24) and Tactics (page 49) offer helpful strategies to try.

Are our expectations realistic?

The difficulties we experience with our children are sometimes based on unrealistic expectations. Thus the parent who feels angry when their two-year-old can't sit still at the table for a three-course meal or who feels their three-year-old should be willing to share their toys with all-comers or who expects their four-year-old never to interrupt an adult conversation is simply demanding the impossible. That isn't to say we shouldn't have any standards. Of course we encourage a young child to sit at the table for a reasonable length of time, we encourage them to share their toys with friends and we expect them to wait a few minutes for our attention when we're speaking but we don't push the child to unreasonable limits.

Difficult behaviour as a response to anxiety and stress

A child who is experiencing distress or anxiety may seem aggressive, destructive or withdrawn. It's not usually very productive to ask a young child if they are worried or upset. They will often not be conscious of what is prompting their bad behaviour. All they know is something isn't right and they are not happy inside themselves. The unfortunate irony of an unhappy child is that when they most need love and warmth they behave in a way that makes them very unloveable and consequently they antagonise the very people on whom they depend for love.

Stress situations
Stress and unhappiness can arise out of all sorts of situations. There are fairly obvious upheavals such as – death or illness in the family, the birth of a sibling, separation or divorce, moving house or starting a new school. Not that every child will necessarily experience stress at these events – some may be comparatively unbothered. But if there has been a major upheaval it can often be the underlying factor in bad behaviour. This isn't to say that we have to accept the bad behaviour but we can perhaps be more tolerant and put greater effort into easing the underlying distress.

A child may be thrown off balance by other situations which are less obvious – a father made redundant, mother returning to work, a best friend moving away, pressure or bullying at school, or parents going through a tricky patch in their marriage. Even when you think you are keeping your worries or difficulties to yourself a child's sensitive antennae will often detect that something is amiss. Even though the child may

have no conscious knowledge of what is happening they nevertheless feel uneasy and anxious.

Although we can't protect our children from difficulties, whenever they become unusually difficult or behaving in an uncharacteristic way we should stop and ask ourselves two questions.

- When did they start behaving in this way?
- What was happening in the child's life or in the family at that time?

You may not be able to do anything to alter the situation. The new baby can't be sent back, you've moved house and you've got to get on with making a fresh start but you can lessen the present pain by acknowledging the child's sadness and by talking over ways you can make things better in the present.

If you think your child's bad behaviour could be triggered by the fact that you or your partner are unhappy or worried then it can help to explain the situation in simple terms. If you tell a child, "I'm a bit worried about things to do with my work. I'm sorry if that's made me a bit impatient with you. You know I love you and things will get better soon." Then the child has some reassuring explanation.

How much to tell

Parental conflicts can be very disturbing to a child especially if they have friends whose parents have separated. A child may imagine a fairly ordinary row could be the beginning of family breakdown. If we are aware of how things seem from the child's point of view then we can give necessary reassurance.

It's a moot point how much we should tell if there really is a serious problem – a life threatening illness or a possible divorce. On the whole it's probably better to withold the more serious information until it becomes necessary for children to know. To saddle them with worrying information that they can do nothing about is to cast an unnecessarily long shadow on their young lives.

Once we can give children an explanation – albeit a simplified one – we can often be surprised at how loving and supportive they are. Providing we don't overburden them with too much knowledge and adult responsibility it is better they have some rational explanation rather than leave them to fear the worst.

Is there something in my child's previous experience or personality causing problems?

Children's own personalities play a considerable part in affecting how they deal with difficulties and influence how we handle them. For example a child who may be naturally explosive or naturally withdrawn and shy will need calming down in one case and encouraging and bringing out in the other. There may also be stages in their development when one of their character traits will create more difficulty. For example the aggressive child may have fiercer tantrums at two than their peers or the shy child may go through a greater crisis when it comes to attending playgroup and starting school.

Earlier experiences can also affect how a child copes with present situations. Thus a child who had a traumatic separation from his parents when he was young – perhaps because a parent had to go into hospital – may be more anxious and clingy whenever a separation seems imminent. This isn't to say that parents should give in to a child's demands all the time. But by being aware of the needy feelings behind a child's behaviour we can put in the extra support that will enable them to work through their anxieties and ultimately increase their confidence and ability to cope with this problem.

Is there something in my past or personality that is making things difficult?

We all have strengths and blind spots. Certain of our attitudes and qualities may mean that we are particularly skilful at handling some problems but we find ourselves impatient or intolerant of other aspects of our children's behaviour.

Am I handling the situation in the best possible way?

When we find ourselves frequently getting into the same conflicts or difficulties with our child it's always worth asking whether there is some alternative way of handling things. Just a slight shift in our approach can sometimes make all the difference. Perhaps by becoming more sympathetic and seeing the problem from the child's point of view, or being more assertive about saying what we want can make all the difference.

Is my child clear about what I expect from him?

Very often we let children know what we don't like about their behaviour without spelling out clearly what we actually expect them to do. How often do we say, "Don't do that" or "Stop it". Or we give vague instructions like "Behave yourself . . . be a good boy . . . eat properly." Older children may understand what we are wanting but younger children may require more specific guidelines such as, "Will you talk normally instead of shouting . . . let your friend have a turn at playing with your trike . . . close your mouth when you chew your food."

Are you under stress?

Problems in our lives can also come between us and the good relationship we normally enjoy with our children.

It's harder to get on with our children if we are stressed, unhappy or don't like ourselves very much. Worries about work, our marriage or lack of self-confidence can all adversely affect our relationship. We are so involved with our own problems we can't seem to find the time and energy to meet our child's needs as well as our own. Some children respond by withdrawing from us. Others will express their anxiety or unease by becoming more difficult.

Do you see your own faults in your child?

Often the qualities in our child that most upset

us and get under our skin are those we least like in ourselves. If, for example, we have constantly struggled against characteristics such as laziness, aggression or shyness we can be unduly alarmed to see these traits reproduced in our children. We may respond by being harsh and critical towards our children partly because we know what a problem these qualities cause in life and partly because we dislike seeing our own bad qualities mirrored back at us.

Does your child remind you of someone else?

Just as we dislike seeing our own negative qualities in our children so we may feel hostile if they seem to be exhibiting tendencies we associate with some other family member – particularly one we don't much like. It's unfair and damaging to label children (either openly or in our minds) as being just like Uncle X or Mother-in-law. Such a label denies a child their full potential and gives them a message that they are not liked or approved of – and for no fault of their own. Every child is a unique person and if we project onto them our feelings about someone else we deny them their individual identity.

Do you give your child a negative label?

One of the most damaging things we can do to a child is to attach negative labels to them. Once we begin to say – or think – "he is . . . out of control . . . a lazy boy . . . hopeless at maths . . . a wimp" or "she is . . . helpless . . . dishonest . . . sulky . . . pigheaded" then we begin to fix a child's development in one particular direction. We cease to see the whole range of possibilities within the child and limit them to one narrow and unattractive possibility. This can become a self-fulfilling description. When a child knows we see them as incompetent, aggressive or whatever then this is how they see themselves and they act accordingly.

This isn't to say we shouldn't be critical of a child's unpleasant or anti-social behaviour but we must distinguish between labelling the child and labelling their actions. Whilst it's all right to

tell a child they are behaving in a way that's lazy, inconsiderate or whatever, it's a different matter entirely to say **they** are lazy or inconsiderate.

Accentuate the positive

Whatever the cause of our bad relationship with our children WE are the adults and ought to be able to bring some sense of perspective to the problem. Hopefully we can make some changes that can lead to an improvement. Even small changes in the way we behave and think about our children can help to shift the emphasis from negative to positive and revive good feelings. If you find yourself out of tune with your child, the following tactics will help to create a happier relationship.

Notice your child's good points

We can easily get into a pattern of only seeing our child's failings. Once we tune in to failings it's as if we become blind to everything that's good in our children. When we find ourselves constantly criticising and carping (whether out loud or just in our own minds) we need to make a conscious effort to reverse the trend.

Decide that, for a certain length of time, perhaps half an hour or an hour at first, you will concentrate on noticing and commenting on anything positive your child does – however small. For example if your child always seems to whine and demands attention, then try and notice just one small incident when he occupies himself. It may only last for 30 seconds but make a point of telling him you are pleased or you think he was very grown-up.

See how this trial period feels. Repeat two or three times a day at first and then increase the frequency of these sessions.

Positive observation has a double effect. It gives you the pleasure of actually saying something nice to your child instead of always having to nag and moan. It makes your child feel better about himself and more willing to cooperate with you.

See things from the child's point of view

When your child is out of the way (perhaps in bed) give yourself time to think about the things you like and appreciate about him. (Look at your child while he is sleeping. It's hard to have negative feelings about a child who's sleeping peacefully!) Think about your child's life: what motivates him and makes him feel good and happy; what frustrates and upsets him. How can you make everyday life better for both of you.

Look forward to the next time you see your child – that may be when he wakes up in the morning or when you collect him from from school or playgroup. Greet him warmly. If you can give out positive happy vibes then you are more likely to get them back. Can you plan a small treat for him, perhaps a favourite breakfast or a detour to the park or cafe on the way home. Or . . . . .

Plan a shared activity

What you plan will of course depend on the age and interest of your child. If, for instance, you are finding it hard to get on with your toddler it will help if you have several novel games or activities tucked away so you can produce something new and interesting next time he becomes fractious or bored. With an older child you might suggest baking a favourite recipe together, or playing a game.

But don't be disappointed if the old niggles flare up. It takes time for rifts to heal and if children are used to relating in a negative way they have to learn new ways to get on together.

Talk to someone who likes your child

Talk to your partner, a friend or relative who knows and likes your child. Encourage them to tell you what they like about your child. Hearing

34

someone else talk positively about our children can help us to see them in a more favourable light.

Share your feelings with your child

Say how sad you are that you don't seem to be getting on well together. Talk to your child about how he feels. Just sharing the sad feelings may help you feel closer or you could brainstorm together about how you can both make things better.

Difficult feelings

No relationship runs smoothly all the time. On occasions we all – ourselves and our children – have to deal with difficult feelings like anger, frustration, jealousy. Many of us find it difficult to deal with strong negative feelings. We may have been brought up to feel it was bad form to make a display of "unacceptable" emotions or perhaps we were often punished for behaving badly. Consequently we learn to suppress anger or put a bright face on sadness and hurt. We may even have succeeded fairly well in keeping our strong emotions under wraps – until we have children. Then the twenty four hour demands of a child often bring these emotions erupting to the surface. We may have to learn new ways of dealing with them. We will also have to help our child deal with their negative feelings.

Anger

Anger is the way we respond to a situation which is causing us frustration, discomfort or pain. Anger can provide a valuable burst of energy which helps us break free from the difficult situation we are in. But it's a risky emotion. It can get out of control and there is the ever-present danger of hurting others. We particularly fear hurting our children. There is also the danger that when we are angry we will expose our nasty side to other people who may reject us or be critical. Thus we often suppress our anger. It doesn't disappear but gets expressed indirectly.

Sometimes this is appropriate. Sometimes it isn't. These are some of the unhelpful ways in which we may express our anger.

- Withdrawing in cold silence. When we are so angry that we cut off communication this is deeply alarming to our children since they feel excluded from our love and affection.

- Going over the top. If we lose control we risk hurting our children either physically or emotionally and we will certainly scare them. The sight of an out-of-control adult is highly alarming.

- Smiling through clenched teeth. People who find it hard to acknowledge their feelings of anger may try to carry on as if nothing has happened, assuming a false cheerfulness. This gives confusing messages to our children who **see** us behaving in one way and **feel** us behaving in another.

- Blaming others. If we find it hard to take responsibility for our own angry feelings we lay the blame at our children's door step, "Look how mad you've made me."

- Internalising feelings of badness. If we feel it's bad to be angry we may assume we are a 'bad person' to have these awful feelings. We struggle with them internally and often become depressed.

Dealing with anger constructively

Learning to deal with our anger constructively helps us to get things changed with minimal damage to our relationship and also acts as a useful lesson to our children. They learn by example how to deal with their own powerful negative feelings.

Positive tactics

One reason why it's so difficult to deal with feelings of anger towards our children is that the balance of power is so uneven. We are strong and they are weak. Somehow we have to cope with our feelings in a way that doesn't abuse our superior strength.

How can we do this?

It's never appropriate to show our anger to a baby or small child. Anger assumes they have some control over their behaviour. However when we do become angry or frustrated with a baby or small child we may need to withdraw from the situation temporarily. Thus if anger is building up when, for example, our baby is crying or our toddler is whining then a few minutes apart in another room – providing it's safe to leave the child unattended – can allow us to release pent-up feelings. It can help to hit a cushion, jump up and down, yell or put on a favourite record.

We can send older children away – into their bedroom or another room – for a few minutes while we calm down.

Another solution with babies and young children is to imagine you're about to go on stage and give a performance of a wonderful mother. Take a deep breath, gather your strength and act for all you're worth. It's surprising how **acting** as if you feel positive and can cope will produce positive results. It also has the effect of surprising your children and taking the wind out of their sails.

With older children

You might be able to avoid the situation arising if you can:

- Give a warning. When you are beginning to feel angry let your child know "If you do that again I'm going to be angry." This is only fair. We can't expect a child to read the signals that indicate an imminent eruption.

- Use I-statements. When you are cross avoid statements that attack your child such as "You are a naughty boy . . . mean . . . horrid . . . a little pest." these only undermine your child and make it harder for you to get on when the storm has passed.

  Instead start by using the word I. "I feel very angry when you shout like that when I'm on the phone. It gives me a headache and I can't hear what Auntie Alice is saying." An I-statement tells the child exactly how you feel and what it is in their behaviour – not themselves – that is upsetting you.

- Be angry with the action not the child. When children do something that makes you angry try and direct your feelings towards the action they have committed (or ommitted) rather than towards the children themselves. Make it clear, for example, that hitting their brother, is unkind or taking money from your purse is dishonest but don't tell a child that they themselves are unkind or dishonest. We need to believe our children are intrinsically good and so do they if they are to develop a positive self-image.

- Act angry. This is not a technique to use too often but it can be very effective when used on selected occasions. Speak forcefully and allow yourself to act angry, give a good performance but still stay in control. Acting angry is often more impressive than going completely over the top. The sight of an out-of-control adult is so terrifying to a child that fear blocks out every thought – they cannot concentrate on what they've done wrong or how they should behave in future.

- Use the whisper technique. At times when your child is shouting or misbehaving avoid the temptation to shout back and thus escalate the aggression. Instead speak to her very quietly. She will have to lower her volume and level of activity to hear you and this will often calm things down.

- Learn relaxation techniques. Many people learn relaxation techniques at ante-natal classes, yoga or through books or television. The trouble is that when we are busy and under pressure bringing up a family, we often feel there's insufficient time to take care of ourselves in this way. Unfortunately, this is when we most need to spend some part of each day calming down and renewing our energies. If you find you are constantly on a short fuse, plan to spend some time – if only 20 minutes – relaxing quitely every day.

- Have short breaks and treats, particularly if you are looking after children alone for much of the day. You might want to enjoy a brief cup of coffee, a magazine, a TV programme, a phone call or a walk round the garden but be sure to build in small treats and rewards for yourself. This can prevent you from becoming too tense and angry.

After the storm

Make it up. If you lose your cool don't leave anger to fester. Once you feel calm again be sure to have a reconciliation. A hug and a chat ensures that the relationship can continue and survive despite angry feelings.

If you think you have been unreasonably angry apologise to your child. You can make it clear that whatever it was in their behaviour that provoked you is still justifiable cause for anger but you are sorry you shouted, frightened them . . . or whatever.

Children's anger

Anger in children is a response to uncomfortable situations such as frustration, pressure, hurt or injustice. The message behind a child's outburst of anger is often something like, "Don't push me around . . . Stop blocking my path . . . Treat me better than this . . . I'm not getting enough love and understanding around here . . ."

As parents we may not welcome our children's outbursts and yet we should rejoice in the spark of energy and assertiveness that fuel the child's anger. That energy is a valuable part of their survival equipment. It's the strength that will help them persevere in life, achieve goals and overcome opposition. Moreover, a child who can become angry is able to stand up for themselves and is less likely to be pushed around or abused by others.

The difficult part for us as parents is responding to the child's anger. We have to object to them hitting out physically or emotionally but in a way that won't destroy their independence and assertiveness. Nonetheless we have to help our children release their anger in ways which don't damage themselves or other people.

The child who never expresses anger should be a greater cause for parental concern than the child who has occasional outbursts. The passive child may be fearful of discharging their anger in which case it is almost certainly being directed inwards. As a result he or she internalises their anger and may feel themselves to be unworthy and bad.

We should try and help these children to get more in touch with their anger. We can point out occasions when anger might be justifiable and give permission for angry feelings, "I should think you must have felt angry when John tore your book like that."

How to deal with anger outbursts

Toddler tantrums

If you feel you've enjoyed a close rapport with your infant it's alarming to find your previously biddable and delightful child turning into a small harridan who throws herself on the floor yelling at apparently minor provocations. What's going wrong? Why is your relationship suddenly deteriorating like this? You've heard of the 'Terrible Twos' but you never thought they'd affect your child.

The two-year-old is beginning to acquire powerful drives and desires. She knows what she wants but when we put blocks in her way and frustrate her desires or we ask her to do something she doesn't want to do then there is nowhere for her driving energy to go. It bursts out in a great explosion of anger.

Your toddler lives in her own world and in the present. She cannot see anyone else's point of view. When she wants something she wants it NOW. She cannot wait and so she flips.

How to deal with tantrums

If your child has a lot of tantrums look at how you can reduce the frustrations and pressures in her life. If you are always saying No or pushing her to do things she doesn't want to do you are making her feel very helpless and creating unnecessary stress. Of course children have to tolerate a certain degree of stress and frustration. We can't give in to them all the time just in case they have a tantrum but if they suffer too much frustration they either become tense and angry or they give up trying. That inner spark dies. They feel hopeless and crushed.

What are the usual areas of conflict between you? Can you do anything to reduce the stress in these areas? If you frequently argue try and involve your child more in choosing what she wants. You may disagree with what your child chooses, but how valid is your objection? For example, you may not want your daughter to go out looking a sight wearing last summer's too-small dress but if she thinks she looks wonderful isn't it important that she's happy about herself? And what will it do for her confidence if you are critical when she thinks she looks wonderful? (The canny parent might however make a mental note to 'lose' this dress at the back of the airing cupboard after today.) Often you can allow the child some choice by asking "Would you rather have A or B."

- Distract. When you see you child heading for disaster draw her attention to something else.

- Avoid unnecessary pressure. Don't put too many restrictions around your child. Don't expect her to behave with a control beyond her years. Remember she is more likely to have a tantrum when she's tired or hungry.

- Give warnings. Don't suddenly interrupt your child or spring things on her unexpectedly. Let her know in advance. "We'll have to leave soon . . . it's your bathtime in ten minutes so we'll have to clear up your toys in a few minutes."

- Weathering the storm. When a child is in the grip of a tantrum stay nearby or hold her to ensure she doesn't hurt herself. Keep calm yourself. A tantrum is a frightening experience to a child.

- Never retaliate. Don't respond by unleashing your own anger as this will only worsen the situation.

- Never give in to a temper tantrum. If a child dicovers she can get what she wants then you reward the tantrum and encourage her to have more in future.

Helping older children

If your child's anger gets out of control and they lash out or break things then sit down with them in a quiet moment and discuss other ways in which they can release their pent-up feelings. They might decide to go into another room and shout or jump up and down or run round the garden three times.

Acknowledge your child's anger. Tell them, "I understand you're angry . . . hurt . . . upset . . . can we talk about it." Being understood can help to defuse some of the anger.

Make it up afterwards when you are both feeling calmer. Have a hug and repair the relationship. Don't harp on about your child's outburst.

Sibling jealousy

Most children grow up with a sibling – either a biological one or a step sibling. The arrival of a new baby can temporarily put a considerable strain on the relationship between the mother and older child. The good news, according to one study, is that deterioration in the relationship between mother and the elder child is short-lived and has usually disappeared within about eight months after the birth of the next child.

From the child's point of view

As parents we like to feel that a new baby will enrich a child's life and be a friend and companion but however much older children

look forward to the new baby they still experience inevitable disadvantages when it arrives. They experience:

- less time and attention from the most important people in their world – particularly mother;
- disruption in the family routine;
- loss of little treats. You may not have time to shop for and cook their favourite food. Family outings may diminish temporarily;
- frustrations when the younger child interferes with their play and possessions;
- the loss of their special position in the family;
- the problem of having to learn to share everything, from your time and attention to the last sausage in the pan.

Given the enormous adjustments they have to make it's not surprising that children show some adverse reaction even if their main response is one of pleasure. In one study nine out of ten firstborn children were reported to be more naughty – defiant, cheeky, and disobedient – after the birth of a sibling. More than half became more tearful and clingy and many showed changes in sleeping, feeding and toileting patterns.

How can we help

A child who is resentful about a sibling is likely to feel angry towards the parents. So there is a double advantage to be gained from trying to make brother and sister relationships as harmonious as possible. There will inevitably be occasional difficulties and bad feelings but the following strategies should help children make the difficult adaptation and minimise the conflict betwen you and them.

- Try to be extra patient and loving with the older child. (This is very difficult when your own energy is at a low ebb but time spent reading aloud when you are feeding the baby or an extra dose of cuddles will give reassurance to the older child.)

- Make special time to be with the older child when the baby isn't around.

- Allow your child to regress and be a little bit babyish from time to time if that's what he seems to need.

- Involve your child in helping with and talking about the baby but be careful not to overdo it. You won't enhance the baby's popularity ratings by pushing her at a resentful brother or sister.

- Encourage your older child to believe the baby likes them. If you can point out, "Look she's smiling at you . . . she likes it when **you** hold her, sing to her," . . . you will help to boost sibling affection.

- Allow your child to ventilate negative feelings towards the baby, "I expect you're feeling a bit fed up with all this screaming this morning." Don't pretend life is sweetness and love all the time.

- Avoid introducing any difficult changes into your child's life around the time of the birth. Starting playgroup, potty training, transferring to a big bed are better tackled well in advance of the new arrival or delayed until things settle down a bit.

Reducing friction

Daily frictions are an inevitable part of family life. He thinks she's taking up too much space in the back of the car. She complains that he's got the flavoured yogourt she wanted. Squabbles between young children quickly get out of hand. She knocks over his Lego tower, so he gives her a push whereupon she picks up the nearest hard object and hits him on the head.

Dealing with squabbles

Some squabbles are virtually unsortable. You either don't see them starting or both parties seem equally to blame. If we try and sort them out we can become entangled in a pantomime chorus of, "She started it . . . No he started it . . . Oh no I didn't . . . oh yes you did" Then ancient grievances are dredged up, "Anyway he smudged my painting yesterday . . . yes but he lost my Snoopy badge." None but fools or saints would try and unravel these diplomatic incidents.

It would clearly be unjust to apportion blame to one child and not the other. In practice the older child is often blamed on the grounds they should know better but this can place an unfair burden of responsibility on one child and store up a lot of resentment. In fact younger children, however innocent they may look, are often quite adept at needling their elder siblings and getting them into trouble. They wind them up then solicit sympathy from parents and sit looking angelic while big brother or sister gets the flak.

Persistent bickering

What most of us find really wearing is the constant squabbling and bickering between children. To change this we have to try and assess the possible causes.

- Are the children bored or left together too long? Perhaps their arguments indicate we should be providing more opportunities for constructive play or we should break up their time together.

- Are they incompatible. Age or personality differences may mean they don't have much in common when they play. In this case we may need to encourage more friendships outside the home.

- Are the children trying to attract our attention? This may sound unlikely but if children learn we come running as soon as they misbehave they will often collude together to stage a scene which will bring us running. Even though we may be angry, negative attention can be better than no attention at all. (See page 50)

Preventing arguments

Research shows that when parents constantly intervene in their children's arguments they worsen the situation. Disputes become more frequent and last longer. The children don't learn how to settle anything themselves and become dependent on a parent to arbitrate and settle all their disagreements.

Whenever possible withdraw from your children's arguments. Tell them it's their problem and they must sort it out themselves. If you normally solve your children's problems they will try and draw you back in. Resist such attempts and make it clear you are not going to be involved. In time you should find your children become more skilful at settling and avoiding arguments.

Sometimes we may have to protect one child if they are at risk from being hurt.

Separation

If children can't sort out their difficulties or they are physically hurting each other then the most effective solution is often to separate them – one in one corner of the room and one in another or if they are old enough they can be made to go into different rooms until they can play peacefully together.

Protecting your peace

There are certain occasions when we have to curb arguments either because they are distracting us, perhaps when we are driving or they are spoiling our enjoyment, for example when we are having a meal.

If children argue when we are driving it can be very effective to threaten to stop the car. If this has no effect we should pull in and refuse to move again until the quarrelling stops. After one or two occasions when you stop in this way children will almost certainly cease or at least limit their arguments in the car.

Similarly, arguments at mealtimes can spoil everyone's pleasure. If this is a recurring problem you can often bring it under control by threatening that they will have to leave the table and go into another room. If the threat alone

doesn't work then insist the children leave and don't return until they can stop arguing. You don't need to get angry or lose your cool. Let the children know you are entitled to eat your meal in peace and you are not going to have it disrupted. When they return to the table carry on as if there has been no interruption.

Partings

Leaving people we love can be a distressing experience. It's one that is particularly worrying for children. It takes time before a child can be confident that mother or father will return. In addition, children experience time differently to us so what is only a short separation to us can seem a lot longer to a child.

A child's life contains many partings – some planned and some not. Some separations are relatively minor ones – leaving our toddler for a few hours with a friend or relative, leaving them at a creche or a birthday party. Yet even these mini separations can be fraught with difficulty and anxiety on both sides.

Children's lives also contain more significant partings – landmarks such as starting with a childminder, beginning nursery or playgroup and of course starting school. Moving house, losing a pet, even losing their comfort blanket or a treasured toy can be experienced as a painful separation by the child. Many children have to deal with their parents separating or divorcing or the death of a close relative.

Separating is part of growing up and we can't protect our children from the pain of separation from us or other loved objects. If we are fortunate we may be able to control the extent and impact of such stressful experiences. If life throws no bad surprises we can help our children separate gradually in controlled stages.

Ideally we try to provide a secure and loving base which will meet most of the child's emotional needs and build up their confidence in themselves and the world outside. When they can trust this security they can begin to venture – gradually – into the outside world.

Small steps and separations pave the way for more significant partings.

Children can exhibit a variety of reactions to separation depending on their age and temperament. Reactions may vary from a cheerful departure with never a backward glance, initial shyness followed by an increase of confidence, loud protest and distress, clinginess and silent withdrawal. Most children will behave in all these ways at various times.

Help your child manage separation

Preparing our children to handle separations with confidence begins early when we encourage them to spend short times away from us.

We can prepare young children in a small way by fading into the background and allowing them to relate to other people – friends and relatives – without our intervention. This enables children to gain confidence in building relationships with others.

If possible we need to separate from our children gradually, allowing them to become confident at each stage before moving on. The stages of separation for a pre-school child might include:

- leaving our child with someone else while we go out of the room and come back a few minutes later;
- leaving our child with someone in our own home while we go out on a brief errand;
- placing our child in a creche while we attend a weekly class (be prepared to spend time settling the child in at first);
- leaving our child at the home of a friend or relative;
- starting playgroup or nursery;
- letting our child sleep away for a night.

When you leave your child

Whether you are leaving your child with a friend, at a creche, with a childminder, at play group or school she is likely to experience some anxiety for the first few occasions. The following strategies will help both of you to cope more confidently.

- Never go away without warning. It may sometimes be tempting to slip away when the child is distracted but only do this if you have first given clear notice that you are about to go. A child who suddenly turns around and finds mother or father has deserted them becomes deeply insecure. They are always looking over their shoulder wondering when you are about to disappear again.

- Let your child know when you will return.

- Spend time settling your child into a new environment. At a creche or playgroup for example go around trying out the toys and equipment together.

- Only leave your child with people in whom you have total confidence. Make sure your child has chance to get to know his carer before you leave him.

- Give your child something they associate with you to look after in your absence – perhaps a hanky with a dab of your favourite perfume, a scarf or a purse.

- Let him know when you will be back – after lunch or in time to share a favourite television programme.

A night away

Children will often have mixed feelings about staying away. On the one hand they look forward to the novelty of staying in a different place and being with their friend or relative but they may get cold feet at the last moment. It dawns on them you won't be there to tuck them up and they won't be in their familiar room. Reassure your child that it's quite natural to miss their home and family a little bit –

everyone does – but emphasise the nice things about being away and express your belief that they will be able to cope alright. If they seem very distressed you can always postpone the event until another time. In this case don't let your child lose face or feel you are disappointed. Be relaxed and matter of fact about the change of plan.

Starting playgroup or nursery

Going to playgroup or nursery is often the first time children go away from home on a regular basis. Most groups will be happy for you to spend time being with your child and settling him in, perhaps over a period of several sessions. If, however, it looks as if your child is going to be tearful and clingy whenever you leave it's often better to make the break and get it over with. Come back again in a short while and gradually extend the length of time you stay away.

If your child cries regularly when you leave it may help if you get your partner or some other close person to take him. Some research show that children who were tearful when their mothers took them to school settled more quickly when their fathers took them instead.

Going into hospital

None of us knows when our child may have to go into hospital. By the age of five one child in four has been admitted to hospital. Half these admissions will have been emergency cases, usually as a result of an accident. When a child is old enough to understand, it makes sense to give them some information about hospitals and medical procedures – just in case.

- Look at books about hospitals and doctors together.

- Take your child to visit a friend in hospital but only if the friend isn't too ill or surrounded by frightening looking equipment. A visit to a friend who has had a new baby can be a positive introduction to hospital life.

- Buy a doctor's kit to familiarise your child with things like stethoscopes and bandages.

- Speak of hospitals in a positive way as a place where people go to get better. If you have had unpleasant medical experiences yourself avoid talking about these in front of your child.

If your child has to go into hospital

- Before the age of two a child will have little concept of what to expect. Between two and five he will be able to take in simple information.

- However difficult or inconvenient, do try to be with your child, particularly in the lead up to an operation and in the post recovery period. Children recover more quickly and suffer less stress if they are supported by their parents. Reassure your child you will be with him.

- Answer questions honestly. A child who is told, for instance, that an injection will hurt for a few minutes and then the pain will go away will be less distressed than a child who is told it won't hurt and then finds he can't trust what you tell him.

- Children often worry that they may never go home again. Make a point of talking about what you will do together when he returns.

- Illness or treatment are sometimes seen as a punishment so make it clear to your child he hasn't done anything bad to cause his illness.

- If you can't answer your child's questions then find out the answers. For questions about hospital procedure speak to or phone the ward sister. For medical matters speak to the consultant or phone the consulant's secretary. The more confidence and information you have the more you will be able to help your child.

Don't be surprised if your child seems very angry with you either during or after a stay in hospital. A child may feel betrayed that you haven't protected them from pain – even though logically this was outside your control.

Or if he has been well enough to enjoy the attention and hustle and bustle of hospital life he may even feel bored and disappointed to be back home. A child's anger or rejection can seem unjust and painful, especially when you have been through a lot of anxiety yourself. Try and see his behaviour as a natural adjustment, not as a personal attack.

Your feelings about parting

From the day they are born our children start to move away from us. Our own feelings about letting go affect how easy or difficult it is for them to say Goodbye. Separation can be as difficult for us as it is for our children. Most of us have felt that lump in the throat when leaving our children on their first day at playgroup or school. And we all know how terribly empty their bedroom can seem the first time they sleep away from home.

There are many reasons why we may find it hard to let go of our children. We may be naturally and justifiably anxious on our child's behalf:

- anxious about their safety;
- worried about how they will cope;
- concerned that no one else will be able to meet their needs or understand them as well as we can.

There will also be anxiety on our own behalf. We may experience:

- sadness that our children are growing up and therefore away from us;
- a loss of role – particularly if our identity is linked with being a parent;
- reluctance to give up some of our control over our child's life;
- fear of the unknown;
- the need to cling to our children to bolster up our own unhappiness or emptiness;
- a re-awakening of our own childhood fears about separation.

Although it's understandable to feel anxiety on our own behalf it doesn't help our children if we hang on to them to meet our needs. Children are quick to detect if we are anxious or unhappy and it becomes very difficult, if not impossible, for them to leave us unless they believe we can survive and cope.

Parents have subtle ways of conveying their own anxiety and neediness to their children. That extra long hug, that anxious inquiry, "Are your absolutely **sure** you're going to be alright?" If **we** can't deal with separation confidently then we certainly can't expect our children to do so.

We must convey to our children an overall impression of confidence: confidence that **they** will be alright and **we** will be alright. That way we arm them with courage and optimism.

The aim of bringing up children is to make ourselves redundant. When our child can walk away from us without too much of a backward glance this isn't a sign of parental failure. It's an indication that we have succeeded. Only when a child's needs have been met and he has a secure base can he begin to venture away from us out into the world where he ultimately belongs.

Divorce and separation

One of the most painful separations for a child is the divorce of their parents, when the family they have always known disintegrates. More than one child in five will see their parents separate before they reach the age of 16. For children, divorce is always a traumatic event. They see their birth family split up and the union which brought them into existence is discarded as a failure. Many children lose touch with one of their parents – usually the father. Children are invariably angry about their parents divorcing. They feel they have been let down by one or both parents. They usually continue to dream of their parents being reconciled long after the divorce, even after one or both of the parents have re-married. Re-marriage itself often brings problems as children have to accept another parent and perhaps new siblings.

The bad news about the effects of divorce on children are well-known but as parents never choose divorce lightly it may be more useful to look at more positive statistics that tell us one child in three appears not to suffer long-term effects.

The factors that can help to lessen the impact of divorce are:

- parents who managed the separation gently with no conflict or fighting over the children;
- both parents continuing to keep close contact with the children after the divorce;
- children being told as soon as possible;
- children being given practical details about what will happen to them: who they will live with, who will take them to school, whether they will still keep their pet dog. Children don't want all the details of the adults' life but they need to know down to the smallest detail how the divorce will affect them;
- reassurance that they will always be loved and cared for by the two parents who brought them into the world. In other words, that although the adults are divorcing each other they are not divorcing the children;
- reassurance that they are in no way responsible for the break up;
- opportunity to ventilate their anger and hurt about the divorce.

Empathic listening becomes vital in helping children express their feelings at highly charged emotional times like divorce. Most will feel great anger and sadness. It is difficult for parents dealing with their own painful feelings to accept their children's grief and rage but the more they can allow their children to release their feelings the sooner the healing process can begin.

Coping with loss and death

The most final and painful separation is death and none of us knows when we may have to help a child cope with a close death. As a society we have become more comfortable with discussing the facts of life but the facts of

death still make us feel very uncomfortable. But death can't be shut out and it makes sense to help children understand something about it from an early age. This needn't be a morbid or frightening process – young children are rarely frightened by death. In fact they are often very curious about it.

Everyday situations provide opportunities for beginning to explain the facts. A dead bird in the garden, the death of a distant friend or neighbour, a walk through a churchyard, all provide an opportunity to talk about death and allow children to ask questions. If we can answer honestly at the child's own level we will be giving important messages that we are not frightened to talk about death.

An understanding of death and its full implications dawns gradually on children. How much they can understand depends on their age. For example a child under three can usually recognise the difference between an animal that is sleeping and one that is dead but cannot yet comprehend that the dead animal will never come back to life.

At around five a child will be getting to grips with the finality of death but there will still be some confusion. For instance they may seem to have understood about granny dying and then ask if she'll be coming for Christmas.

Plain speaking

In an attempt to cushion their children – or themselves – from the reality of death, parents may use euphemisms such as 'falling asleep', 'gone away'. Such terms can cause problems. It's not uncommon for a child to develop a phobia about going to bed or to become extremely anxious if a member of the family goes away simply because sleep or departure have become associated with death.

The way we explain death will depend on our child's age. It can be helpful to ask children what they think happens when someone dies. This will give us a useful indication of any misconceptions. For example many children think death is violent or is a punishment for some misdeed.

Preparation

For many children the first introduction to death is the loss of a pet. It can be very tempting for us to try and avoid their distress by dashing out to find a replacement for that gold fish that floated to the top of the bowl or not to admit that the cat has been run over but to pretend it has strayed. This may make things more comfortable in the present but we are denying the child an important rehearsal for more painful experiences later in life.

Given an opportunity, children can find consolation in devising some funeral ceremony for a family pet. Burial, picking flowers and saying some special words can help them come to terms with the loss.

A close death

One of the difficulties for children when there is a close family death is that not only does the child have to deal with their own confused feelings but they are also exposed to the distress of other people. Suddenly all the grown ups who represent their security are crying or withdrawn. Everyone is wrapped up in their own grief and doesn't have time to give to help the children.

Comforting a bereaved child

Let them express their feelings

Avoid the trap of telling a child "Don't cry . . . it'll upset mummy or daddy." To damn up their tears is to prolong the process of mourning. The more we can allow our children to express their grief the better their chance of recovery.

Young children may be helped to express their feelings through drawing or painting.

Dispel feelings of guilt

Children may suffer from irrational feelings of guilt after someone close to them dies. They sometimes feel it's their naughtiness or angry feelings that have caused the person's death. If we can explain why the person has died and emphasise that it is no one's fault, the child can be released from their guilt.

Talk about the dead person

Keep the memory of the dead person alive by talking about them and looking at photographs. But avoid creating an over idealistic picture. A perfect person can turn into an impossible role model.

Explain that the hurt will not last for ever

A child who is grieving themselves or who sees their parents grieving should be told that grief is normal. They should also know that it won't last for ever. The sad feelings will go away eventually.

Don't misunderstand indifference

It's not uncommon for a child, when told of a close death, to carry on playing as if nothing has happened or they may speak of death in an apparently callous way. The child may not be old enough to understand the implications of death or perhaps their self defence mechanism shuts out the unacceptable, only allowing it to penetrate gradually.

When to get help

A child who becomes withdrawn or very disruptive for any length of time may need professional help in coming to terms with their loss. A family doctor should be able to advise about local counselling services.

How to discipline your child effectively

Discipline and guidelines

Every child needs guidelines and limits to give shape and security to their lives. Limits are a kind of behavioural map which says "You can go this far but no further (at the moment)" Parents who would never dream of dumping their child down in an unfamiliar town or countryside and leaving them to find their way about unaided often feel reluctant to provide a map or guidelines about how to get about in everyday life.

As parents we must believe we have the right to lay down some limits and exercise our authority. Otherwise our children walk all over us; they are unable to learn to self-discipline and they don't learn how to behave or how to get on with other people. As far as possible we try and discipline our children in a way that shows our respect for them as people. We involve them as much as possible in taking some responsibility for decision making since, ultimately, they have to learn self-discipline. It also makes sense to be positive in the way we control our children in order to maintain a good relationship with them.

However, there are some matters which are simply not negotiable and we shouldn't be embarrassed to stand firm and insist that our child complies. If our relationship is fairly warm and democratic on the whole then the occasional, "Because I say so," will not do any harm.

Obviously limits and rules shouldn't be repressive so that children feel trapped and helpless. Guidelines should also be reasonably consistent so children know where they are from one day to the next. A few clear and fair guidelines create the balance between the child's need for security and their need to develop into individuals who can make some decisions for themselves.

Some limits are in the interests of our children's safety:

"Don't play with matches."
"Hold my hand when you cross the road."
"Always let us know where you are going when you go out."

Some rules are aimed to protect our space and preserve OUR sanity:

"Keep your cassette player low early in the morning."
"Seven o'clock is your bed time."
"Don't leave your school bag in the hall where I fall over it when I come in."

How to discipline your child

Our own discomfort about setting limits means we often don't do it very well or with enough conviction. The following guidelines are pointers for setting limits effectively and fairly.

- Speak with conviction. When you ask your

child to do something – or not to do something – believe in your right to set limits. Speak firmly and believe your child should do as you ask. Our children quickly sense if we feel uncomfortable, apologetic or unconvinced and naturally enough they won't comply.

- Give clear guidelines. Vague instructions leave too much room for interpretation and disagreement. We should know what we want and convey it to our children clearly.

  The following vague statements don't give children sufficiently clear indications of what exactly we are asking them to do:

  "I wish you'd help me sometimes."
  "Behave nicely."
  "Should you be watching television now?"
  "Tidy your bedroom."

  These statements are open to interpretation. The child is left wondering . . .

  "What exactly does mother want me to do to help her . . . and when . . ."
  "So what's wrong with how I'm behaving at the moment . . ."
  "Why shouldn't I watch TV now there's a good programme on . . ."
  "But I've tidied my books off the floor."

  We should know exactly what we want and spell it out. The above statements might translate more specifically into the following instructions:

  "Will you put away the shopping and stack the dishes."
  "Stop hitting each other in the back seat."
  "You've already seen the programmes we'd agreed on so the television must go off now."
  "Clear all the things off your bedroom floor and hang up your clothes."

- Be honest. Don't pretend you are offering a choice when you aren't. "Would you like to tidy your bedroom?" or "How about washing up?" may sometimes be presented as optional suggestions but it's unfair to give the illusion of asking when we are in fact telling.

- Use positives where possible. If you are always saying, "Don't . . . stop it . . . you can't" children feel they are always being criticised and got at. This makes for resentment and lack of co-operation. Turn negative statements into positive one's wherever you can. The following examples show how a negative command can be re-worded more positively,

  "Don't eat with your mouth open."
  "Please eat with your mouth closed."

  "You're not having a biscuit until you've cleared up your paints."
  "You can have a biscuit when you've cleared up your paints."

  "Don't push your feet into your shoes like that."
  "Look after your shoes by undoing your laces before putting them on."

  "You can't watch television all evening."
  "You can see an hour's worth of television this evening. What would you like to choose?"

- Let your child know the reason for rules. Children are likely to comply more willingly if they understand **why** they are being asked to do something.

- Be fair and reasonable. Avoid giving too many instructions and be sure your expectations are realistic. If you set too many limits or too high a standard children will become resentful.

- Be reasonably consistent. We aren't robots and we are never going to be completely consistent all the time but children don't know where they are if we are furious about something one day and let them get away with it the next.

Tactics

The ultimate aim of bringing up children must be to help them take control of their own lives

49

and their own behaviour. Although we may have to be fairly directive in the early stages of a child's life it's worth bearing in mind that we are aiming at developing self-discipline. So it's a good idea to help children understand first of all what is wrong about their behaviour: "It gives me a headache when you shout like that." or "Other children won't want to play with you if you don't share with them." It then helps to try and involve the child as far as possible in working out the solution to the problem – some ideas are outlined below.

When children understand what is wrong with their behaviour and how to put it right they have useful tools which will help them work out future problems. Moreover they learn to think of themselves as able and coping. They feel better about themselves and they are less hostile to you. Solving a problem cooperatively does minimum damage to your relationship.

'Naughty' behaviour: understanding what's going wrong

The first step in finding a solution to problem behaviour is to stand back and look at precisely what's happening when things go wrong.

Most situations have three phases which we can label **ABC**.

A is the Antecedent or the context in which the event occurs.
B is the child's Behaviour.
C is the Consequence or the pay off. It's what happens or what a child gains as a result of their difficult behaviour.

To see the **ABC** formula in action let's consider two scenarios from everyday life.

Scenario one: the tantrumming toddler

Every time a two-year-old child reaches the supermarket checkout she screams for sweets. Her mother resists but when the screaming is particularly ear-shattering she sometimes gives in and buys a packet.

In this scenario:

A the antecedent is the situation of child and mother shopping and reaching the super-market check out.
B the behaviour is the child's tantrum and screaming.
C the consequence is that the child some-times achieves her goal but only when she's screamed particularly loudly.

Scenario two: the squabbling siblings

A brother and sister frequently start squabbling aggressively when they play together. Mother rushes in and tries to sort out the problem. Each child accuses the other of some offence. Mother gets thoroughly tied in knots trying to sort out the rights and wrongs of the situation. Ten minutes later the scene is repeated again . . . and then again . . .

In this scenario:

A the antecendent is the two children playing together
B the behaviour is the squabbling that breaks out
C the consequence is that mother comes on the scene and gives her undivided attention to the children

In many problem situations parents try and intervene when the things have reached the **B** stage, when the child is screaming or the siblings are squabbling. It's often more productive to consider whether we can intervene at point **A** or **C**.

Changing the antecedent

In the case of the tantrumming toddler the mother can look at what she can do **before** she gets to the checkout or even **before** she gets into the shop. Her possible options are:

- shop elsewhere;
- shop without the child at least for a while;
- come to some agreement with the child beforehand. She might agree some

acceptable treat that is conditional on the child not screaming at the check out. If the child still screams the mother would have to explain to her daughter that she was breaking her agreement and the 'treat' would be forfeited.

In the case of the squabbling siblings it clearly isn't feasible to stop the children playing together though the mother may consider:

- not leaving the children to play together unsupervised for so long or she might sensitise herself to early signs of brewing trouble and intervene before a full scale row erupts;
- come to some agreement with the children about how they behave to each other. She might agree to take them swimming or have a favourite meal if they play together without fighting.

Changing the consequence

When we look at what happens at point **C** in our two scenarios we have some clues as to why the children continue repeating their undesirable behaviour. When the mother gives in and buys sweets the toddler receives the pay off she wanted. In other words she is rewarded for her tantrum.

Even though she doesn't succeed every-time, the reward comes with enough frequency to encourage her to continue. She's a smart child and learns it's worth persevering and she knows the greater disturbance she can make the greater her chance of success. Most of us would willingly stand and scream in a supermarket queue if we knew this could achieve our heart's desire.

The pay off for the troublesome siblings is that they get mother's attention. True, it may not seem very desirable to have a cross mother but that can be better than no mother at all. Moreover, if they're bored, then tying mother in emotional knots can be wonderfully diverting. Children can collude together quite unconsciously to manipulate adults and bring them running.

It may seem bizarre to imagine that a child would want to make a parent cross. But children desperately need our attention and if we don't give it voluntarily they'll extract it from us in any way they can. And if naughty behaviour produces a reaction from us then that's often preferable to no reaction to all.

Negative reinforcement

In each of these cases the children's bad behaviour has been rewarded. In one case it is rewarded with sweets and in the other by maternal attention. Rewarding bad behaviour is called negative reinforcement. It has the opposite effect of what we want to achieve. It encourages children to continue with the undesired behaviour that we want to get rid of.

Alternative tactics

How else might parents have responded at the C stage of the situation in order to have weakened rather than strengthened their child's undesired behaviour? They might have:

- ignored the bad behaviour. It will take considerable time for the supermarket parent to discourage the screams because the child has come to expect some refusals but knows it is still worth persevering;

- punished the screaming or the quarrelling perhaps by withdrawing some treat;

- made some intervention which ensured the squabbling children didn't do each other any mischief but which didn't give them the pleasure of her attention. For example if she had separated them she could have ensured they were unable to argue again in the immediate future.

It would of course be unreasonable to expect a toddler never to have a tantrum or siblings never to quarrel. Such behaviour is natural in both cases. It only becomes a real problem when it occurs frequently. It's the frequency that tells us we obviously aren't handling things effectively and should look for some alternative way of dealing with the problem.

Stick or carrot

When we are trying to encourage 'good' behaviour in our children and discourage 'bad' behaviour we have two main options. We can either use the stick approach and discourage the undesired behaviour through ignoring, telling off or punishment. Alternatively, we can use the carrot approach and reinforce the desired behaviour through rewards which might be tangible rewards or social rewards such as approval.

Positive reinforcement

Discouraging undesirable behaviour alone can make for a very negative relationship. We also want to encourage and reinforce the positive things our children do. Positive reinforcement is good for our child's self esteem and makes for a warmer relationship. Children get good feedback from us and don't feel we're always going on at them. In addition we have the pleasure of giving out praise instead of feeling we're always nagging. As a result both parent and child feel more confident and successful and happier with each other.

Good feedback

We are often more tuned in to our children's bad behaviour and weaknesses than we are to their strengths and good behaviour. We criticise the one and take the other for granted. The outcome is that children become discouraged. They have no incentive to behave, to be helpful, to play cooperatively or work hard if those behaviours are never recognised. It can have a powerful effect on children's behaviour if we can make LESS fuss about – or even ignore – undesirable behaviour and give MORE recognition to desired behaviour.

Looking for good points

To see how effective this can be try and step up the positive reinforcement you give your child. But first observe your own use of praise and criticism. Which do you resort to most frequently? During a short period of time such as a meal, a trip in the car, or an outing to the shops make a note of the number of times you use negative reactions – critical, correcting or cross statements or tone of voice. Notice how often you use positive reactions – an encouraging or appreciative statement, a warm tone of voice or a smile.

A self-observation made during the course of lunch for example might include some (though hopefully not all) of the following negative reactions:

Negative statements such as:
"Don't talk with your mouth full."
"Don't reach across the table like that."
"Stop kicking your chair."
"Hold your spoon properly."
"Don't spill your drink."
Non verbal negative reactions such as:
a cross tone of voice;
a sigh;
a frown;
raising your voice;
slapping;
withholding food.

Positive reactions observed over a meal might include:

Positive statements such as:
"It's nice to see you enjoying your lunch."
"I like to have a good chat when we eat together."
"You're very grown up these days."
"You ate that so well perhaps you'd like second helpings."

Non verbal positive reactions such as:
a smile;
a pat on the shoulder;
a warm tone of voice;
offer of more food or favourite food.

Whenever we find some aspect of our child's behaviour is annoying us it's worth making a point of looking out for the opposite side of that behaviour. For example, if we're fed up because our child is unhelpful and moans everytime we ask them to do something we should be alert to any occasion, however small, when they actually do something without a moan and then give some recognition, "Thank you, I appreciate you doing that."

You may feel, "Why on earth should I praise my child for something they jolly well ought to do naturally?" In the long term you don't want to get stuck having to praise your child for every little thing they do. But it's only while you're at the inital stages of shifting your child's behaviour that you need to resort to slightly exagerated encouragement. Once your child's behaviour has improved you will only need to reward with positive comments and rewards from time to time.

Reward systems

So far we have mainly considered social rewards; approval, a friendly word or a pat on the back. For problems that have become habitual and need a more conscious effort from the child we might decide to offer more tangible incentives and rewards. The kind of difficulty that might be helped by a formalised reward system could be:

- never tidying up;
- not doing homework;
- using bad language.

Star charts

Draw up a chart with spaces to record the child's success with a tick or drawing. A young child will love to have spaces in which they can stick peel-off stickers when they are successful. There should be an agreed reward for an agreed number of stickers. Young children need to have their interest maintained by receiving a small reward frequently, probably daily. With older children you should be able to negotiate a longer term reward. Rewards should be appropriate to the age and interest of the child. They shouldn't be discouragingly difficult to achieve but neither should they be achieved without some degree of effort.

Rewards for a pre-school child might include a favourite item of food, an extra story, an outing, a game or a small toy. Older children will normally be happy to accumulate their tokens over a week to trade them in at weekend perhaps for money, an outing, a toy or piece of equipment, staying up later or watching a favourite television programme.

How long should incentives be used

On the whole a reward system will have achieved its aims within a few weeks – or at the most a few months. It should always be seen by both parties as a short term incentive and not a means of extorting goodies for life. Of course even when you've abandoned the rewards scheme it's a good idea to give occasional rewards or recognition.

Parents sometimes fear that giving rewards will turn children into young mercenaries who put out their hand whenever they stir themselves to make an effort. Provided this is a system you use occasionally and for a short term there's no reason to assume children will be corrupted by a reward system.

Make your child more responsible

However effective reward or punishment systems may be, in the long-term we want children to take responsibility for their own behaviour. Telling our children what to do trains them to do as they are told but not to think for themselves.

Involving the child in the solution

Children are capable of coming up with ingenious solutions to their own problems. When we ask a child to contribute towards the solution of a problem we are showing them respect and expressing our confidence in their ability to think and behave in a mature way.

Brainstorming

Brainstorming is a creative and democratic way to try and solve a problem together. This is how it works:

- Sit down with everyone who is involved.

- Have a large sheet of paper in front of you.

- Outline the problem and how you feel about it. It might be,

  "Every morning you dawdle through breakfast, take ages to get dressed, can't find your bag and we end up rushing to school in a mad panic. That puts us all into a bad mood with each other and makes me late for work. I don't want this to go on any longer."

- Invite solutions. It doesn't matter how bizzarre they are. Don't criticise any ideas at this stage, encourage free thinking. Write down **every** suggestion.

- When you've run out of ideas then go through the list. It may include:

  lay out clothes ready the night before;
  hire a maid;
  work out a time table;
  give a ten and five minute warning before departure;
  take the mornings off school;
  pack bag the night before;
  Mum to give up work.

  Everyone has a chance to comment on all the suggestions. The impossible ones are edited out. From the remaining solutions you all agree on the suggestion or suggestions you want to try.

- Write it down and place the new plan in a prominent position so there can be no arguments about what has been decided. Because the child has contributed to the solution they now have more vested interest in making it work. Even quite young children can be involved in brainstorming. Brainstorming encourages children to see themselves as problem-solvers not just problem-makers.

Learning from cause and effect

While children are very young it's our responsibility to care for them and protect them from suffering the outcome of their actions. For instance we harness them into their high chair and baby buggy to prevent them falling or throwing themselves out. As they grow we continue to care for them but gradually hand over more responsibility.

Sometimes, out of habit or anxiety, we continue to do our children's worrying quite inappropriately. Thus we rush around the night before the school PE lesson washing and drying the kit they've just fished out of their bag at the last minute. Or when they've raided the fridge without permission and eaten the food we'd bought for their tea we feel we have to put ourselves out to get them something else. By doing this we prevent our children learning from the consequences of their actions.

It's easier to hand over responsibility for some things than others. For instance we may not feel able to see an expensive bike go rusty when our children forget to put it away but we may feel there is less at stake in encouraging our child to organise their sports kit. However, if we intend to hand over responsibility to our child we must be fair and give clear warnings and reminders. We should tell them that we are no longer responsible for this particular problem and they must look after it for themselves in future. After that we must be prepared to stick to our word.

It's also important to choose a time when failure wouldn't be utterly devastating. You can't, for instance, allow them to be late at a time when they are sitting exams or they might miss the school bus and be at risk if they had to get to school under their own steam.

It can be very difficult to stand firm and not rush to the rescue. For this reason we should only threaten what we know we can carry out without putting our child at risk. We must be prepared to let them fail or forget initially – and this can be hard for both of us. If for instance you have made your child responsible for remembering to produce their PE kit in time for washing or if you have made them responsible for getting themselves ready for school on time you may watch with a sinking heart when they go off with soiled kit in the morning or when they are seriously over-running their time.

Avoid getting cross or agitated. It's not your problem remember. The child will learn their lesson from the inconvenience they have created for themselves, not from your wrath or anxiety.

Keep calm and bear with the failures. Refuse to take any blame. After suffering the inconvenience of their failures once or twice the child will shoulder their own responsibility and an area of struggle and nagging will have gone out of your life.

Avoiding hassle

There are several useful tactics we can use to reduce hassle when correcting our children. They make the child feel we are treating him more fairly and responsibly and produce a more positive response.

Appeal to the child's positive side

If we tell our child "I know you're a kind boy . . . you were very brave when . . . you're good at . . ." we are confirming our faith in them and encouraging them to draw on their existing skills to deal with the problem in hand. Children are more receptive to suggestions that they improve or correct their behaviour if they feel you basically like and approve of them.

Explain the reason

If we are wanting our child to behave differently we should make it clear why. Whether you're asking them to put their clothes away at night or to speak to you more politely they should be able to see some pay-off for the desired behaviour. The pay off might be, "You won't have a last-minute panic every morning hunting for clothes" . . . or . . . "You'll find we get on much better together when you're pleasant."

Use impersonal statements

Whenever you are using "You" statements turn these around to an impersonal statement. For example instead of: "You must go to bed at eight o'clock" try, "Eight o'clock is bed time." Or instead of "You should eat your vegetables." try "People eat vegetables to keep healthy."

The impersonal statement carries authority and takes the subject out of the arena of personal confrontation.

Give a warning

When your child is doing something wrong, warn them that you are going to take some action. For example you might say, "If you bounce that ball in the sitting room again I shall take it away for the rest of the day." Or, "If you don't stop arguing by the time I count to five, you'll both have to go up to your room."

A warning gives a child specific notice about the penalty he must pay if he continues his behaviour.

Use positive statements

How many times a day do we say "Don't"? Try and ban the word from your vocabulary for a short time. Change negative instructions to positive ones. For example, instead of saying, "Don't spill the water," you might try, "Carry the water carefully so that it doesn't spill." Or turn the negative instruction, "Don't shout" into "Do speak more quietly."

Telling stories

Children will often respond more readily to a story than to directly being told how to act. For example, if your young child seems antisocial and never shares her toys and upsets other children who come to play, you might tell her a story about another child or even an imaginary animal who wouldn't share. You might stop and ask the child, "What do you think this character should do about this?" Let the child suggest a solution and incorporate it into your story. Seeing our faults and hearing a solution through a story is less threatening than being lectured on how to behave directly.

Role reversal

This can be very effective with young children. They often like to play the mummy or daddy while you are the child. Use this situation to feed back to them an impression of their own behaviour. If you act in a clinging or whining way your child will begin to understand how their behaviour seems to you. But allow the child to absorb the implications without pointing out the connecton. If you say to them, "This is how you behave" . . . or, "how do you like it." they are likely to feel uncomfortable with the game and not want to continue.

Know when to turn a blind eye (and a deaf ear)

Canny parents know that it really isn't worth taking issue with every little thing our children do wrong or life could turn into an endless inquisition or battle ground. There are times when it is better not to see your youngster dip their finger in the jar of jam, nor hear them mutter about your shortcomings under their breath. (We all do things that we prefer other people not to see or hear. The only difference is, as adults we're more skilled at keeping things hidden).

Avoid no-win situations

Don't get into conflicts you can't win. There are some things you can never force your children to do, such as eat, sleep or say something they don't want to. We put ourselves in a very weak position if we demand something we have no power to enforce. A battle of wills which the child wins is no good for anyone.

Allow opportunity for children to make amends

If your child has done something wrong which he or she may regret, help them to put things right or say sorry. This can be much more healing and effective than punishment.

Use humour

If your child is very forgetful and you find yourself constantly reminding or nagging then try humour. Notes or acting will bring your message to your child's attention in a light-hearted way.

- Make your points with notes or drawings. For instance if you want to remind your child to clean the bath after themselves you could stick a picture with a sad face over the bath saying, "It's not much fun to bath in scum."

- Ham acting is particularly effective with bad habits such as awful table manners, sucking fingers or picking noses. If you imitate the child's behaviour in a wildly exaggerated fashion they will usually laugh and get the point without you having to say a word.

Punishment

Much as we hope our children will behave well through encouragement and example there are inevitable occasions when children don't co-operate or they break the rules and we have to take some actions.

Punishments that are not too severe and that are only administered occasionally will not damage our relationship. They show our children we care about them and we have some standards we are not prepared to compromise.

Punishment must vary according to the age of the child and the offence committed. Punishment is **never** appropriate for babies or very young children. Punishment assumes the child understands what is expected and has the ability to control their actions. If we need to control very young children – perhaps we want to stop them hitting out at another child or crawling towards the electric socket – then we use distraction, a firm warning "No" or we physically remove them from the situation.

Punishing children either involves taking

57

away something they want or asking them to do something they don't want to do. There are some things which should always be a child's inalienable right and which should never be withdrawn whatever they have done. For instance we may choose to withold a treat ice cream or sweets from our child but the right to join a family meal is something that should not be denied them. We may separate them temporarily from our presence but they should never feel that we don't love them or that we reject them.

On the whole punishment should always:

- Be a last resort. Only when we have tried positive means of persuasion or when the offence is very serious should we resort to punishment.

- Follow closely on the crime. The sooner the punishment follows the crime the more effective it is. If possible you should try and catch your children red handed since it is more effective if they are stopped while they are actually committing the crime. In addition, the sooner the punishment is over the sooner you can become close again. If you threaten your child that they have to miss a favourite television programme this evening or they cannot go on an outing at the weekend then you will both live under a cloud for the rest of the day – or longer.

- Be fair and not too severe. If your child feels you have been unjust or unreasonable then their anger towards you will outweigh any regret at their own action. If you threaten too severe a punishment you are less likely to carry it out and will lose your credibility with your child. An unnecessarily harsh punishment will cause resentment.

- You should give clear warnings. A child should know exactly what's at stake before

they transgress. If you are feeling unwell or fragile then let the child know you are on a shorter fuse than normal.

- There should be a clear and definite limit to the punishment. No child should be expected to endure parental wrath and disapproval indefinitely. Once the punishment is over try and establish close contact again. Don't bear grudges. This doesn't negate the effect of the punishment. It shows that you continue to love the child even though you disapprove of what they have done.

- Be calm and matter of fact. A punishment should underline the child's failure to comply with a sensible rule or principle. It should not be a personal attack on them nor seriously disrupt your relationship. You may even want to express sympathy with the child at times, "I'm sorry you have to miss your programme. I know it's tough but I gave you a warning and you chose to ignore it."

- It should be seen as fair by the child. A child will feel very resentful if they are punished for something which their siblings or visiting children are allowed to get away with. Sometimes the elder child feels hard done by if they know others in the family are not punished. In this case always make it clear to them why you are not punishing the others. The older child should also feel they have some compensatory privileges.

- Don't punish twice. If a child has been punished by one parent or at school they shouldn't be punished again.

- Make the punishment private. A child should not feel publicly humiliated by their punishment. It lowers children's confidence and self-esteem if they lose face with others. If you have to tell a child off when you are with other people – for example when you have visitors or are staying with other people – then take the child outside the room or to some private space. Then help make their re-entry into the group as easy for them as you can.

What kind of punishment?

Make the punishment fit the crime

As far as possible we should aim to make the punishment have some logical connection to the offence committed. It should also relate to the child's understanding and ability. Thus, if we see a two-year-old throwing stones at a window for the first time we may indicate this is a serious offence by our tone and the severity of our warning but it would not be appropriate to punish the child. They are not old enough to have known the outcome of their action. In fact we may be at fault for not having provided adequate supervision. However, a six or seven your old throwing stones at a window should understand the implications of their actions and may deserve punishment.

Deprivation

A child may lose privileges or possessions as a means of punishment. If, for example, they are mistreating a toy you might take the toy away for an certain amount of time. If a child consistently makes a mess of their clothes, changing several times a day and leaving discarded clothes crumpled on the floor, you might argue that they cannot have a choice of clothes until they prove they can look after them better. You would then remove all but one or two outfits from their wardrobe and gradually replace their other clothes when they can prove they are able to look after them.

Loss of television time can be an effective deterrent. A proportion of pocket money may be withdrawn for a serious offence but it's rarely effective to withdraw pocket money for longer than one week. The idea of giving children money is to help them learn to budget and this lesson cannot be learned if money is cut off at source for any length of time.

Loss of attention

Withdrawing our attention can be a great deterent to bad behaviour. We may tell a child,

"I'm very cross about what you've done and I don't want to talk to you for the next five minutes." Other family members must also withdraw attention. Withdrawing our attention is a relevant way of punishing a child who has misbehaved socially – perhaps moaning, whining, being aggressive. If we are feeling very cross this tactic also gives us time to cool down. But it's important to mark the end of the withdrawing time and to create an opportunity for reconciliation.

Time-out

Time-out is a more formal way of depriving a child of attention. Time-out is most effectively used for anti-social behaviour – hitting, shouting, aggression. The child is taken by the adult into an unstimulating part of the home – the hall is often a favourite place. (Some people use the bathroom but this is full of potential hazards and seldom appropriate.) He is told to stay there for a short period of time – about 3 minutes for a pre-school child and 5 minutes for a child of 5+. A kitchen timer may be set to indicate the end of the set time. If the child attempts to come out of time-out or misbehaves while he is in time-out then the time is set back to the beginning. Time-out is used most frequently with pre-school and primary aged children.

At the end of time-out the child should be called back into the room, when you both carry on as if nothing has gone wrong.

Don't send a child to their room or to bed as a form of time-out. The child's room should be an inviting place where they can feel relaxed and secure when they go to bed. It shouldn't become a punishment centre.

Making amends

A constructive way of punishing bad behaviour is to help the child make amends. If, for example, they have deliberately broken another child's toy you might suggest giving up something of theirs in reparation or perhaps they should contribute towards a replacement out of their own pocket money.

If children are helped to understand the impact of their behaviour on the other person you may encourage them to say sorry or write a note of apology. However, there is nothing worse then an insincere apology so this option has to be judged carefully.

Another form of making amends is having to perform some act to put things right. Thus if a child has been consistently warned against walking into the house with muddy boots, you might, after giving due warning, insist they clean the kitchen floor. If you make sure this is done as thoroughly as the age of the child will permit the chances are they will be far more careful in future. This sort of punishment is positive in that it teaches the child the direct link between their action and its consequence.

Telling off

Telling a child off is one of the most common ways of correcting behaviour. Reprimands should be used sparingly since children just switch off or begin to feel negative towards an adult who is always scolding.

There are several clear steps to giving an effective reprimand:

- Point out the behaviour that must be changed, "Don't interrupt when I'm talking."

- Explain the reason, "I can't have a private conversation."

- Tell your child how you expect them to behave, "Wait until I've finished talking, or, if it's urgent say This is an emergency, can I speak now."

- Tell you child what the penalty will be if they carry on interrupting.

- Check your child understands the message by asking them what you have told them.

Punishments to avoid

Don't yell or shriek at your child. It is frightening for children to see their parents out of control

60

and the child is too alarmed to focus on what you are saying.

Don't make children feel guilty. If children are made to feel guilty they are storing emotional problems in later years. Comments like, "After all we've done for you . . . how could you do this to me . . . you'll be the death of me" can put enormous emotional burden on children.

Don't threaten a child or try to coerce them by anxiety; threatening to call in some external authority such as the police, or threatening to abandon the child creates great anxiety.

Physical punishment

Hitting children is an option fraught with dangers. It can easily cause injury, either physical or psychological. In addition it doesn't appear to be particularly effective. Research suggests the more children are smacked the less notice they take of it.

Smacking, when it is a short tap on the hand of a toddler crawling towards a plug or some other danger, may act as a kind of aversion therapy when other tactics such as distracting or using a strong No have failed you.

Other kinds of smacking or hitting undermine a child's sense of self-respect. Children know physical punishment is unfair since it is an abuse of your physical power and they cannot reciprocate. Hitting and smacking don't teach children how to solve their problems peacefully and children who are hit are more likely to resort to violence to get themselves out of difficulty. If we sanction the use of violence for ourselves we can hardly object when our children resort to the same methods.

But one of the greatest dangers of physical punishment is that it can so easily get out of control. A smacking given in anger can have a force which the angry adult cannot fully appreciate. And when this smack doesn't work the temptation next time is to smack harder and so violence escalates.

Winning ways with common problems

we expect our children to share their toys with a visiting child who wants to take over their ride-on truck and play with their dolls, it's equivalent to us allowing someone into our home who then helps themselves to the contents of our cupboards, takes our car out for a test drive and then takes over our children. Would we really like that?

Many parent-child conflicts arise because we ask children to do too much too soon. We expect them to exhibit a level of control and understanding that are beyond their reach. They fail and feel frustrated.

The more we can be firm but relaxed and see things from the child's point of view the better we can guide our children and still remain good friends with them.

Eating problems

One of the most common difficulties between parents and children centres around food. Parents worry that their children eat too much or too little or they don't eat the right things. Food plays an important part in all our lives and has a powerful emotional significance. When we hold a new baby in our arms it is totally dependent on us for its survival. We are responsible for making sure it receives enough nourishment to develop and grow. This can feel like an enormous responsibility. We begin to worry about feeding our children and the anxiety can continue for years.

Giving food is symbolic of giving and receiving love. In the early months of life, feeding, if it's going well, can be a deeply satisfying and intimate experience. Parents feel good because they can meet their child's needs and the baby feels close and loved. Conversely, if things don't go well, if parents find it hard to feel close to their children or there are feeding difficulties, they may have a sense of guilt and failure. If babies reject the parents' attempts to feed them or the growing child doesn't want to eat the meals that have been prepared then parents can feel angry or distressed. Their love

Learning to fit in

In the process of growing up children have to master many physical skills, from feeding themselves to crossing the road unaided. They must also learn complicated codes of behaviour; when to say please and thank you or that, although mummy says you must always tell the truth, she gets upset if you tell someone they are fat or bald. There's a lot to learn and it can often seem confusing.

In order to fit in with our routine and with other people, children have to curtail many of their own powerful needs. In the long run this is in their own interest. The child who can't restrain him or herself or get on with others is in for a lonely time.

But we shouldn't underestimate the difficulty of what we expect. For instance, when and care are being rejected. Parents sometimes withhold food to express their lack of love for their children.

Feeding our children is a very basic way of demonstrating our love and care. Therefore, when children don't eat what we have provided and prepared we often have two sets of response. We are concerned for our child's physical well being: is he being adequately nourished? We may also respond on an emotional level, feeling angry, hurt or frustrated that our effort to give seems to be rejected by the child.

Most of the time the child is simply responding to his own body messages. Many children have erratic eating patterns. Their bodies go through spurts of growth. They may be very hungry and wolf everything you put in front of them for several days, or weeks, and then become disinterested in food for a while. In many ways this is perhaps more natural and in tune with their body rhythms than our habit of eating three meals a day regardless of whether we are hungry.

Doctors always say that if children are healthy and active then their bodies are getting all the nourishment they need. If you aren't sure or your child seems listless then it's always worth compiling an eating diary over several days and taking that to your doctor or health visitor.

Putting undue pressure on a child will cause them to dig in their heels. Once children get a merest whiff of parental anxiety they will use food to assert themselves – to gain your attention, to worry you, to annoy you and generally play you along. You are into a power struggle which you cannot hope to win because there is no way you can force a child to eat.

The only way to survive is to separate out the health aspect of food from the emotional and refuse to play the emotional game. Don't get upset and angry when your child refuses food – be fairly matter of fact. If you have spent a lot of time preparing a meal then it can certainly feel like a slap in the face to have it rejected but the child doesn't usually see it this way and this is rarely their intention. One answer is to invest less effort in cooking – at least for the time being.

Getting them interested

If you are worried that your child isn't eating enough there are various subtle ways of encouraging them to take greater interest and feel more involved in family meals. Try the following tactics:

- Let her help you choose the menu.

- A young child might enjoy drawing the menu on a menu card, her blackboard or as a picture to go on the fridge for the rest of the family to see. Having some proprietorial interest in the meal can make her more disposed to eat it.

- Involve her in laying the table. Perhaps she'd enjoy decorating place mats, folding napkins, putting some flowers in a pot or laying out place names.

- Give small helpings that are easily managed (with the option of coming back for more) rather than overfacing her with large portions she can't manage.

- Put serving dishes in the middle of the table for people to help themselves. Many a child who'll refuse something when you offer it first time will eventually reach out to help themselves when they see everyone else pitching in.

- Encourage your child to enjoy cooking.

- Providing a range of different foods from an early age will make it easier for your child to feel more confident when they eat out.

- Avoid talking about slimming or losing weight in front of your child. Children can become conscious of the importance of their shape at an alarmingly early age.

The wrong foods

If your children eat too much of the wrong kinds of food or demand sweets and biscuits between meals, then you can try these tactics.

- Make the fun food conditional on eating up something else, "You can have a biscuit when you've eaten your dinner."

- Don't stock the problem food in the house if it means your child is always nagging for it.

- Discourage eating between meals and if children insist they're hungry then just allow them something plain and uninspiring.

- Teach your child the basics of nutrition. Encourage them to see food as something they eat to build up a healthy body. If they understand they need to have some protein, carbohydrate, dairy produce, fats and fresh fruit or vegetable with every meal they can begin to take an interest in and responsibility for their own eating.

Sleeping

Few, if any, parents survive their children's childhood without having some sleep problems – and some feel they have more than their fair share!

Children need differing amounts of sleep and have different sleep patterns. Some get into a routine effortlessly. Others need a lot more time and help before they establish a regular sleep pattern.

There is a variety of attitudes about children and sleep. There is the point of view that claims children should be allowed to fall asleep and wake whenever they choose. Then there's the point of view that believes parents should establish a strict sleeping regime and ignore the child's demands for attention and comfort in the night.

The trouble with the first course of action is that it deprives parents of any time they can confidently call their own. And eventually the child is going to have to adopt reasonably conventional sleep patterns in order to stay awake for playgroup and school.

The second approach seems heartless in expecting a small child to be cut off from the security and comfort of their parents for a large part of their 24 hours.

In practice most of us muddle along, finding some sort of compromise between the child's needs and our own. The most common sleep problems are children not settling at night and children waking at night and demanding attention.

Not settling at night

We all know the delaying tactics children can adopt – another a drink, a last story, another cuddle, clinging, crying; you can find it takes ages to extricate yourself and then the shouting for more goes on for the rest of the evening. If you totally ignore the child they can become deeply anxious and fearful about whether they've been abandoned. If you go up and meet all their demands then you become increasingly exhausted and resentful.

The best tactics for settling children down in the evening are:

- Make sure they have had enough exercise to be tired but not over-tired. If they are too tired or excited, children find it hard to relax enough to get off to sleep.

- Establish a regular bed time routine – perhaps bath, story, tuck up, cuddle, and goodnight. Make this enjoyable but fairly low key so the child can gradually wind down.

- If children continue to call down when you have left them they are either wanting more entertainment or they are anxious that you might not be there and they are checking up on you. Although **you** know you wouldn't abandon them, fear of abandonment is a deep and natural fear.

You need to offer reassurance in a way that doesn't also provide stimulus and entertainment – otherwise you'll be kept busy all night.

Be prepared to go back into them or to call goodnight but don't get drawn into any activities, songs or long cuddles. Switch off and be utterly boring. Don't get your children out of bed or you teach them that it pays to persist

with calling out. Eventually your children will get the message that you are there and they can feel secure but they learn there are no interesting rewards. Be prepared to keep this up until they get bored. It may take several weeks but the frequency of demands will wane and eventually stop.

Make noises – open and close doors, do some ironing or clearing up activity on the landing or in the hall where the child can hear you. Put on a radio (the television might be too inviting). Create a sense of your presence in the house. Children's anxiety can often be triggered if the household suddenly goes silent. In an attempt to create quiet conditions for sleep we may inadvertantly be worrying our children and giving them cause to feel we are no longer around.

"I can't get to sleep."

Children may worry if they don't get to sleep quickly. Our instructions yelled up the stairs, "Get to sleep" probably don't help much. We all know the more you tell yourself to go to sleep the more wide awake you become.

Instead explain to the child that everybody takes a little while to get off to sleep and in fact we normally go to sleep when we are thinking about something else. Discuss with them some nice things they can think about while they are lying in bed.

If your child seems unduly worried about not sleeping then take the pressure off them by telling them you want them to see how long they can stay awake. Suggest they keep their eyes open and stare at the ceiling. They mustn't get out of bed but when they call down to tell you they're still awake – then congratulate them. Tell them they're doing very well to stay awake for so long and just to keep staring at the ceiling. This tactic can take the anxiety out of not sleeping.

Waking at night

Having got your child to sleep, this only solves half the problem. Neither you nor they have any control over whether or not they will wake at night. When young children cry out at night

we obviously have to check that they are alright. We may have to go through the settling routine to reassure them that we are around. From about the age of three we can explain to our child that everyone wakes up at night but they just lie quietly until they go back to sleep again. Unless we tell them this children don't realise that what is happening to them is quite normal. It might help if you discuss with the child what they can do when they wake up. Perhaps there is a teddy they can cuddle. If they don't like the dark perhaps you can agree to switch on a low light for them when you go to bed.

The family bed

In many cultures parents expect to share their bed with their children or the children sleep altogether in the same bed. It's largely a matter of your own instinct and convenience whether or not you want to bring your child into bed

with you. It's very often easier to feed a child at night in the comfort of your own bed. But later on it can be difficult to reclaim your bed for your own exclusive use once your child has staked a claim.

If you want to stop your children coming into your bed during the night you obviously don't want them to feel rejected. It's probably unfair to move them out too suddenly but you can accustom them to go through the night in their own bed using the following guidelines.

When they wake go into their room and settle them down there. If they get up and come into your bed either move them back into their own room when they have fallen asleep or go straight back to their own bed with them. Have a cuddle in their bed to help them settle down.

They can still enjoy a cuddle in your bed in the mornings.

Is your child ever rude and bad mannered?

At some time or other most of us have sat open-mouthed while our child lunged across the table to seize the last piece of cake from under our nose, or uttered some offensive word or phrase we didn't think they could possibly know. All children are rude and bad mannered at times.

But let's face it, adults don't always set the best example. We interrupt when children are speaking, we don't listen to what they are saying, or we make comments about their personal appearance. When the boot is on the other foot though, we're quick to find fault and condemn.

The best foundation for good manners is to treat our children with courtesy and consideration. And what isn't caught in the way of good manners we need to ensure is taught. Manners are not a social frill but an expression of respect for oneself and others. They make everyday relationships warmer and more enjoyable. A child who has been helped to understand these principles and act on them will feel socially confident in many different kinds of company. On the other hand the child who is abusive, insensitive towards others or who eats with all the grace of a waste disposal unit is destined for a lonely life.

Get to the root of the problem

There are a number of reasons why children behave rudely. Once we've recognised the underlying cause then it's easier to tackle the problem effectively.

They don't understand what's expected

The world must seem a confusing place to young children. There are so many new things to learn and what's all right in one context may seem rude in another situation. For example it's all right for a child to ask for a biscuit or say he's hungry when he's at home or at granny's house but grown-ups get uncomfortable when he says this at other people's homes. Expressing his needs is perfectly natural to a young child but as he gets older he will have to learn this isn't always appropriate.

They lack social skills or are embarrassed

A young child is often too shy to say thank you, especially with unfamiliar people. The teenager may burst into a room where his parents are talking with friends and completely ignore the visitors because he is feeling gauche and awkward. When we recognise that our child is acting from embarrassment and awkwardness we can help smooth their path. We can say thank you on behalf of the toddler or introduce our son and help him into the conversation with a friendly comment.

They are releasing anger or frustration

Bad manners are sometimes an expression of a child's anger. Of course we must put our foot down and say we don't find their behaviour acceptable but then it's worth addressing the underlying problem, suggesting, "I think you might be feeling angry or upset about . . ."

They are showing off or seeking attention

When children feel undermined or unimportant they will try and grab attention by whatever means they can. They may learn we notice them when they misbehave and ignore them when they behave. Showing off is more likely to occur when there are other people present or if they are being egged on by someone else.

They are imitating behaviour they've seen elsewhere

If children see other people getting away with certain kinds of behaviour we can't really blame them for having a go themselves.

They are over excited

There are occasions, perhaps at a party, when children's manners slip a bit.

How to correct bad manners

We obviously want our child to learn social skills in order to fit in with other people. But we need to help them acquire these skills in such a way that we don't undermine the child's self-confidence or make them painfully inhibited and anxious about always putting a foot wrong. The following ways of correcting bad manners should help keep our children on the right tracks.

- Show good manners to our children. Example is the best teacher.

- When they misbehave don't attack the child themselves. For instance we might point out, "You're behaving very rudely" rather than "You're a very rude boy."

- Coach them tactfully beforehand if you know they are likely to forget themselves. For example, if they are going to have tea with a friend you might chat to them on the way about why it's nice to say "Thank you" when they leave.

- Don't let the child lose face. Making our children look small or silly will undermine their confidence. If a child is behaving badly in company it is often better to take him outside and have a word with him. Then help to ease him back into the gathering.

- Step in to smoothe his path. If a young child is too shy to answer or speak up, try and help him get his message across.

- Be clear and firm about where the limits are, "I'm sorry that's just not on."

- Help your child say sorry. Some children find it far more difficult than others to apologise when they've done something wrong. Help a reluctant child by showing your appreciation when they apologise . . . and be prepared to apologise to them when necessary.

Bad language

All children flex their verbal muscles and experiment with unattractive language at some time. Even very young children will sometimes pick up inappropriate expressions from older siblings and friends. A low key response is usually the best way to deal with this age group. If you simply ignore the expression or tell them it's boring they usually lose interest very quickly. However if they still persist (perhaps because they are being encouraged by an older sibling) then you have to explain that this upsets other people and they are not allowed to say it.

On the whole, if we over-react to a word or expression we endow it with power and it becomes the child's secret weapon – something they can trot out to disconcert us at inappropriate moments.

With older children there are occasions when we simply have to tell them "I don't want to hear that again." But, in fairness, we should remember that words which have offensive connotations for us don't necessarily have the same meaning for children. The best way of deterring children may be to explain the significance of what they are saying.

Every child is experimenting with behaviour and language and they will inevitably make mistakes from time to time but if we can point them in the right direction and believe in them they're unlikely to go far wrong.

Untidiness

Tidiness or lack of it is a frequent source of irritation between parents and children. We all have a different level of tolerance and it's unrealistic to expect children to be unduly tidy. Young children particularly are exploratory by nature and over-emphasis on tidiness can inhibit their learning. On the other hand, too much chaos can be equally inhibiting if children are surrounded by disorder and cannot find things when they want them.

It saves a lot of hassle if we can encourage our children to tidy away from a reasonably young age. Of course we can't expect very young children to clear up after themselves unaided, but if we always let them get away with sitting by while we rush around after them they will never feel responsible for taking care of their own things.

Motivating young children

We can encourage young children to help tidy up in the following ways.

- Tidy up together and make it enjoyable by chatting, singing or playing some music.

- Challenge them to a race against time. Set an alarm to go off or aim to complete the job by the time a cassette tape ends. Or you could race to see who can clear their corner of the room first.

- Don't start one activity until a previous one has been cleared away.

- Make a treat conditional on clearing up. For example when you have cleared up you will have a drink and biscuit or read a story together.

Older children

Older children will know from experience that untidiness can be frustrating. They can't find their things or there isn't room to do some particular activity because everywhere is too cluttered. Make sure children understand the reasons for being tidy.

Encourage older children in the following ways.

- Be specific about exactly what you expect when you ask a child to tidy up. Stand in the room with them and point out what has to be put away. Don't ask them to do too much at once. They shouldn't be overfaced with an impossible task.

- Make a checklist of the tidying jobs you expect them to do either every day or once a week. For example, a daily list might include: put away school bag, hang up coat, put clothes away, clear bedroom floor, put out clothes ready for tomorrow. Such a list is particularly helpful to children who find it hard to get organised in the morning. They will find it easier to start the day when everything is to hand.

- Make a regular treat, such as a television programme, dependent on having cleared away. Give prior warning.

Untidy bedrooms

When your child is young you will obviously take care of their room together but as they become older they will come to feel increasingly territorial and see their room as a private space outside your jurisdiction. To maintain minimal standards of hygiene you may choose to make certain rules, such as no food to be left in the bedroom or the room must be cleaned through at agreed intervals.

But by the time your child is into early adolescence you clearly shouldn't have to constantly chivvy him to keep his bedroom tidy. By this stage you should be able to close the door and ignore the muddle. It's his problem not yours. If you can be strong-willed and endure this, in time most children discover the disadvantages of chaos for themselves and will make efforts to be tidier.

Your problem

Even though we can turn our back on our children's untidy rooms because that is their problem and not ours there is no reason why we should have to tolerate chaos throughout the rest of the house. One drastic, but fairly effective, solution is to gather their scattered things into a cardboard box or bin bag and put them out of the way – in an outhouse or under the stairs. Tell the child you will throw away anything that hasn't been claimed and put away by the end of the week.

Untidy bedrooms may sometimes affect us when our children's friends come to play. Because of the lack of space or because they can't find what they want they tend to mooch around being bored or else they spread themselves through the rest of the house. If you find this is a problem then you could have a rule that friends can't come round if the bedroom is too untidy to play in. It's amazing how one or two disappointments will quickly make a child ensure their room is in a reasonable state.

Taking care of yourself

needed to fetch and carry, and be available to support, talk and be a general guide and friend.

However much we enjoy being with our children we need to have some separate life we can call our own. We need time to work, time to play, to develop our own interests and skills, to be with our friends and our partner and time for our own re-creation. And yet we often feel guilty looking after ourselves. We may prefer to put other people first and put ourselves last. But we do ourselves or our children a disservice when we fail to meet our own needs.

We should look after ourselves for the following reasons.

- We have to renew ourselves in order to regain the physical strength to look after our children. We can't keep drawing on our reserves without replenishing our lost energy. It's not in our interests or our children's interests if we are constantly exhausted.

- We need to take breaks in order to feel mentally and emotionally refreshed and to be more lively, happy and a more rounded person.

- If we totally dedicate our lives to our children we are in danger of feeling tied and eventually becoming resentful towards them.

- Children who are the sole *raison d'etre* of their parents' existence carry a heavy emotional responsibility. Parent and child can become too enmeshed and it's difficult for the child to become fully independent and separate from their parents. Children sense when their parents are emotionally dependent on them and they can experience this as a heavy responsibility.

- Our children must learn that they are not the centre of the universe, and other people count too. If children are accustomed to parents always being at their beck and call, dancing attendance, they will find it difficult to form equal relationships as they grow up.

- Children learn to develop their own resources if they can't always call upon us.

Why you need to take care of yourself

Until we have children ourselves, none of us can fully anticipate just how much of our time and emotional energy they consume nor just how draining their demands can be. It often feels as if there's precious little of anything left for ourselves. As small babies our children need care and attention day and night. As they get older we can gradually hand over more and more responsibility to them as they begin to feed themselves, dress themselves and look after their own things. Eventually our children will go to school on their own, prepare their own lunch-time sandwiches and organise their own homework.

Although we may do less for our growing children in terms of physical care we are still

70

- If we have a partner then we need to protect our time together. It's ultimately in our children's interest that we maintain a strong relationship.

Much of the time we are coping with a juggling act, trying to balance all the different aspects of our life – our own needs for peace, pleasure, time; our children's needs for attention; our work; our partner; family; friends. We often find these elements in conflict. For example, we want to sleep but a howling baby can't be ignored in the early hours of the morning; our partner has arranged to take us out to spend some time together but the babysitter cancels at the last minute and we can't go out; an important work meeting coincides with our child making his first acting debut as an angel in the school nativity play.

Our own needs inevitably take second place a lot of the time but we have to ensure they don't take second place ALL the time. If we don't take care of ourselves there's a danger that we become exhausted, angry and resentful. We do a disservice to ourselves and our children by turning into a martyr. When did anyone enjoy the company of a martyr?

Make time for yourself

Making time for yourself when you are bringing up small children is never easy and yet it's in everyone's interest you make this a priority. Try and ensure there's some time you can count on for yourself every day. When looking after babies and small children it's often necessary to snatch odd minutes whenever we can. The trouble is there are so many things competing for our attention that, unless we put ourselves on the priority list, our own needs get overlooked. When our baby or toddler takes a nap for example, we may be tempted to dash around trying to catch up on our work but this time may be better used to give ourselves a break.

'My time. Your time.'

As children get older we may continue to feel we have to be constantly on call. Yet even a toddler can be trained to respect the fact that

mum or dad sometimes takes a short break with the paper or a cup of coffee. If you haven't got your child in the habit of accepting your right to occasional peace and quiet then begin to train him. Use an egg timer or a kitchen buzzer and let him know he can't bother you until time is up. Be realistic and don't expect more than three to five minutes peace from a toddler initially. Promise you will play with him or give him attention when you have had your turn at doing what you want. Children who are unused to entertaining themselves will find this arrangement difficult at first but you will both benefit ultimately. You will establish a right to time for yourself and your child will become more self-reliant as he learns to occupy himself for short spells.

If we make a point of claiming some time for ourself it's easier to be more whole-hearted and positive about the time we give to our child. The worst of all worlds is when we never claim time for ourselves nor give it enthusiastically to our children because we feel grudging about all the demands they make. As a result we may be with our children physically, but be mentally or emotionally absent. We only listen to them with half our mind and we are disinterested in their company. We don't get what we want and neither does our child since our response to them is at best half-hearted or at worst grudging.

When we protect our own interests and make time for ourselves it is much easier to give more willingly and warmly to our children. Far from being selfish we are taking better care of both of us.

As our children get older it often becomes more difficult to protect our time and privacy. They start staying up later. Our teenager wants to fill the house with friends at all times and may ambush us late in the evening with fraught questions about whether or not they can go to a disco at the weekend.

It can be difficult to strike the right balance. We want to support our children but we also feel the need to protect ourselves from late-night demands and confrontation. One solution might be to declare a curfew hour – a particular time in the evening which is 'our time' after which we don't want to be harassed with loud music or bothered with problems.

Something just for you

If we are to enjoy spending time with our children and looking after them we will almost certainly have to give up some of the interests and social activities we enjoyed before they were born. However, it's inadvisable to let go of all our activities outside the home. We will soon come to feel tied and unstimulated. Whatever the effort, it pays to make sure we do some things in the week solely for our own pleasure – whether it's keep fit, further education classes, learning a musical instrument, a sports activity, or just meeting with friends.

Doing something apart from our family gives us an important sense of identity and a change of perspective. Even if this proves difficult in the early days, it may be possible to organise reciprocal babysitting arrangements with a friend or find some activities which have creche facilities attached.

Care for yourself

Once we start handling a family budget it's amazing how difficult we find it to spend money on ourselves. Too often we become the Cinderella of the family, happy to spend out on everyone else but closing the purse when **we** want anything. It's bad for our morale and nobody will thank us if we are always at the bottom of the family priority list.

You will need to take care of your morale when you are looking after children. If you allow yourself to become drab and dowdy you will feel and behave as if you are drab and dowdy. When you are constantly giving out love and care to others don't forget that you need attention too. Know what makes you feel good about yourself – it may be a good haircut, a facial, a massage, exercise. Whatever it is, make sure you meet some of your own needs. You cannot give out all the time.

Review your priorities

Before having children you may have enjoyed working, running a well organised home, knocking up amazing menus, or making your own clothes. But unless you find these activities therapeutic or vital to your life there's a better chance of maintaining your health and sanity by letting go of unnecessarily high standards and by taking short cuts. Perfection and children just don't go together.

Do you do too much?

Children are always changing and developing, which means we also have to change and adapt as parents. As our children increasingly become more competent and self-reliant, so we can begin to claim back more time and energy for ourselves. But we sometimes cling to outdated parental obligations and responsibilities long beyond the point where they are necessary or desirable. We may, for example, still be spoon feeding our two-year-old, dressing our four-year-old or preparing our teenager's lunch at a time when they can do these things for themselves.

There are many reasons why we may find ourselves undertaking inappropriate caring for our children. Perhaps:

- We've failed to notice our child's increasing competence and respond appropriately.

- We feel it is the **duty** of a good parent to do everything for their child. (In fact it is the duty of a good parent to enable their child to grow increasingly independent.)

- Our children make us think it is **our** duty to do things for them. Children will quickly catch on to any guilt in us and use all the tactics at their disposal – sulking, wheedling, moaning, shouting – to make us do things for them.

- It may save time and trouble to do things

ourselves. Letting children take responsibility initially requires more time and patience. We have to be prepared for them to make more mess when they learn to feed themselves, to take a long time when they dress themselves or we have to spend time teaching them how to prepare their own lunch but short-term inconvenience pays off with long term rewards – our children become more capable and we have a little more freedom.

- We want to feel needed. It can be difficult to hand over autonomy to our children if we feel reluctant to give up our role as caregivers. Such feelings can be a sign that we are investing too much of our own lives in our children and need to develop our own separate interests.

Over the course of a day or two, notice the things you do for your child and consider whether you are doing too many things she should be doing for herself. Perhaps your child is now old enough to put her own toys away, fetch her own coat from the hall, clean out her own lunch box when she comes home from school or wash her own hair.

If you find yourself feeling resentful at some of the tidying and clearing jobs you have to do; picking up clothes from the bathroom floor, wiping up when your child spills things or hunting for their lost shoes, it may be a sign that your child should be taking more responsibility for these things herself. Similarly, if you are always having to intervene in disputes or entertain your child when they are bored it may that you are allowing your child's problems to become your problem.

If we allow ourselves always to be summoned like the genie of the lamp to meet our child's every desire we are creating an impossible slave role for ourselves. We are not doing our children any great favours either since we're standing between them and their growth towards independence. We probably also notice that we get little thanks for doing slave duty. In fact the more we do the more children expect us to do. The more we try and solve our children's problems and ease their path the more we find ourselves blamed when things go wrong.

Of course there are times when it's appropriate to spoil our children a bit. We happily do them good turns when they're tired or under pressure and enjoy helping them out. Our children will appreciate us taking special care of them at these times if they haven't come to regard spoiling as the norm.

"It's your problem"

When we feel our child is leaning too heavily on us we should make it clear that some tasks are going to be their responsibility in future. Then we must detach ourselves and let them get on with it. It may be difficult at first to tell a child "You must find your own lost toy . . . I'm not going to clear up after you . . . you must sort out your own arguments and not coming running to me every time." Initially, children may protest at having to take responsibility but if we don't expect them to handle too much too soon they will gradually become more self-reliant when they see we are not going to rescue them all the time.

As a parent it can be wonderfully liberating to say, "That's your problem . . . I'm not going to do it for you." Once you realise that you no longer have to be responsible for everything your child does, or doesn't do, a great weight falls away. You can still care for your child and feel sorry for their difficulties but you simply refuse to pick up the burden and carry it around yourself.

Are you hung up on guilt?

It's amazing how quickly we assume every difficulty in our children's lives is our fault. If they find it hard to settle down at playgroup, have difficulty learning to read, are not the most popular child in the school we instantly ask ourselves, "Where have I gone wrong?" We worry we may have been too patient, not given them enough time, that we haven't fed them properly or provided a sufficiently creative environment.

It's as if we carry an invisible label around our necks saying, "Whatever goes wrong I must be guilty." Somehow we have to try and come to terms with the fact that no child and no parent is perfect. We all experience difficulties in certain areas of life. That isn't anyone's fault or cause for blame. That's how life is.

How to beat guilt

Next time you catch yourself thinking about all the things you haven't done for your children, pause and think about all the things you **have** done.

And if you decide you would like to make some improvements don't get hung up on what you see as your past failure. Instead, look upon the future as an opportunity for a fresh beginning and make practical plans for ways in which you can change things. Don't expect wonders of yourself – a small adjustment which you keep to is better than some Grand Design which collapses after a few attempts and only leaves you feeling more guilty.

For instance, if you think you don't spend enough time talking with your children or you worry you don't provide a sufficiently creative environment then see how you could make some practical adjustments to improve these situations.

When it comes to spending more time talking you could look at the everyday opportunities you aren't using to the full at the moment. Perhaps you could use the trip to school to become more aware of your child. Or use bath-time as a relaxed occasion to chat.

Making a more creative environment can require more determined action. You may have to plan to have some corner where your child can make things and perhaps review their materials to see where you can make additions or replacements. In addition you might decide to go to the library and borrow some

stimulating books. Finally, you may plan to make things or carry out some specific projects together.

In this way you can turn guilt into positive action. And if you don't feel you can do anything about the situation then you might as well stop feeling guilty about it!

Different circumstances

We bring up our children in a wide range of different 'family' situations. There is the traditional family of mother-father-and-children, parents living apart with shared custody, adopting parents, foster parents, single parents, step-parents. Each family situation has its own rewards and pleasures and its own difficulties.

Within the family set-up, parents may work inside the home or outside the home. Again there are disadvantages and drawbacks to each of these choices.

Working at home or working outside

The degree of choice we each have about our particular situation has a significant impact on our level of satisfaction and affects the success of whatever arrangements we make. So a parent who has **chosen** to work outside the home is likely to be happier, more fulfilled and committed to making their system work than one who is going out to work from necessity. Similarly a parent who has **chosen** to stay at home is likely to be happier than one who is staying at home because suitable outside work isn't available. It's having control over our lives that helps us feel positive and happy. Lack of control makes us unhappy, guilty or discontented.

If we are unhappy with our situation, it makes sense to review our decision. What might have seemed the right decision at one time in our lives may not be the right option now. If we are in the difficult position of not being able to change what we are doing – we want to work but can't get a job, or we are working and can't afford to give up, then we may be able to lessen our unhappiness by developing a more positive outlook and seeing the benefits and advantages in what we do and focussing less on the drawbacks and disadvantages.

Staying at home

Parents who stay at home with their children can enjoy being closely involved in their child's learning and development. They can enjoy all those significant first steps and avoid the anxieties of organising childcare and having to leave a child who may be ill or unhappy. The downside of full-time parenting can be boredom, isolation and frustration and the continual round of unstimulating chores.

Anyone looking after a child full-time needs social networks in order to ensure a break from the unrelieved company of children. This is particularly true of single parents who cannot look forward to the arrival of a partner bringing an external perspective on life as well as practical and emotional support at the end of the day.

Support networks

Some people have family or a close group of friends and neighbours who can be called upon but first-time parents particularly may find themselves isolated. They now have a different lifestyle and interests to the friends and colleagues they knew when they were childless. The very act of becoming a parent can be isolating, limiting your access to other people. It's not so easy to get out and your time and energies are taken up with looking after your children.

It may therefore be necessary to set yourself a deliberate task of making contacts and finding friends. A parent's best resource is other parents. From them you gain support,

information, understanding. You might explore the following possibilities.

- Join local parents and baby or toddler groups (your Health Visitor should be able to tell you what groups meet locally. If you are new to an area your Health Visitor may also put you in touch with another mother of similar interests to yourself.)

- Join any adult education classes that have a creche attached.

- Get talking to other parents informally wherever you can – in the supermarket, at the clinic, at playgroup, nursery or school. Be prepared to make the first move with anyone you feel could be a potential friend. If you feel shy about asking them round for a coffee you always have the excuse that the children can play together.

- Get someone to introduce you to the local babysitting circle.

Have some structure

One of the things you may enjoy about being at home with your child is the freedom to make up your own routine and to please yourself. But sometimes this can become uncomfortably unstructured. There seem to be no markers in your day and one day is indistinguishable from the next. If this bothers you then it may be helpful to work out some kind of pattern to your days and weeks. This can provide a sense of organisation and motivation.

Living with chaos can become demoralising so if possible it makes sense to have at least one room in your home – perhaps your bedroom which is an adult haven. Make this a luxurious place where you can withdraw to relax and escape from the hurly burly.

Working outside the home

Parents who work outside the home may enjoy increased financial independence, stimulus, a sense of personal satisfaction, social contacts and an avoidance of feeling lonely or trapped at home.

The other side of the coin is exhaustion at juggling the demands of children, home and family, regret at missing some of the important moments in their child's life, the stress of dealing with crises and **guilt**.

Guilt

Guilt is probably the main emotional problem for working mothers. We feel guilty that we aren't spending enough time with our children (particularly if they are ill). When we are with our children we feel guilty we aren't giving enough of ourselves to our work, our partner, our home, our friends. Whatever we are doing we are conscious we ought to be doing something else. Our best never seems to be quite enough and we seem to be constantly running to stand still.

To survive we have to take a realistic picture of what is happening in our own and our children's lives. Provided children have good alternative care there is no evidence to suggest they suffer when both parents work. Some parents notice distinct **advantages**, both for themselves and for their children:

- children have a wider social network;
- they are more independent;
- daughters of working mothers are more likely to have high ambitions for themselves than the daughters of non-working mothers;
- mothers have an increased range of interests;
- there are greater material benefits;
- women who feel they lack the patience to stay at home all the time feel they enjoy their children more and are better parents just because they have a break from them.

What kind of childcare?

The most important decision for the working mother is to arrange the kind of childcare that will best suit her child and her own working circumstances. Children must have care that offers security, continuity, affection, understanding of needs and appropriate stimulation. Time, effort and research spent on finding the right care for your child and your circumstances are vital if your child is going to be happy and you are going to work with peace of mind.

There are pros and cons for every kind of care which you will have to weigh up very carefully.

Day nurseries

These have the advantage of usually opening throughout the year and offering care for long hours. Many are well equipped. They provide opportunities for children to learn to socialise.

The disadvantages are they are few and far between and you may have to travel some distance. If there is a rapid turn over of staff children may suffer from lack of continuity. If the nursery gives priority to children from deprived families there may be an unduly high level of children with behavioural problems.

Work place nurseries

The advantage of these are they are usually close to your work so you are always at hand during the day.

The possible disadvantage is that if your work is some distance from your home your child may be involved in a long journey at the beginning and end of every day.

A childminder

The advantages are she is usually a mother herself working in her own home and can thus provide a close substitute for family life. Usually there are other children, which provides opportunities for your child to socialise. With care, you should be able to find someone with similar attitudes and approach to childrearing as yourself.

The disadvantages are that she may be ill, go on holiday, leave the area or stop minding and you will have to find alternative care at short notice. She may not be able to look after your child when he is ill.

Live-in nanny

The advantages are, flexible care, especially if you want someone to cover for odd hours or to do some evening babysitting. Your child is in his own home. When the child is ill there is someone to look after him.

The disadvantages are, you must give up some space and privacy in order to have someone living with you. Live-in nannies are an expensive option. Your child may lack the stimulus of playing with other children.

Day nanny

A nanny who works in your home but who doesn't live there may not be able to provide the same flexible hours but you won't have to share your home with another person.

Sharing your child's affection

Many mothers worry that their child will love their minder more than themselves. In practice this is rarely a problem. If your child is pleased to spend time with someone else this is a plus in their lives and a sign that you have made a good choice on their behalf. However, this doesn't take away from their pleasure at seeing you when you return.

You and your partner

It seems an irony that a child who is the expression and result of a close and intimate relationship between two people should often create a rift between those same two people. No matter how much you both adore your child, feel enormous pride in your joint creation and share wonderful moments of tenderness as you rejoice in her achievements together, her very existence also puts enormous strains on your relationship. We have considerably less time and energy to give each other and there is the ever-present danger of drifting apart.

Some research finds marital satisfaction drops after the birth of a baby. Couples find a little more satisfaction with each other when the children are of primary school age. This drops again when children reach adolescence and couples only regain their former marital satisfaction when children leave home.

Parents have less time to be alone with each other. You are constantly interrupted – even in the middle of the night – and there are never enough opportunities to feel close and talk together. The adjustment from being a two-some to being a threesome puts you under emotional, physical and financial strain.

Make time for each other

It is too easy to let children take over but your relationship with your partner is not only important to you, it is important to your child as well. The loving support of two adults who are also loving and supporting to each other provides stability and security for a child. You owe it to your child, as well as to yourselves, to make your relationship a priority.

Finding time for yourselves has to be a conscious decision. It will rarely happen by accident. If you find it difficult to get yourself organised to go out, you may find it a good idea to book a weekly babysitter then you are obliged to get out and spend time together. Even if you only go to a pub to sit and talk you have one guaranteed 'togetherness' slot in the week.

You should also accustom your child to the idea there are times when you want to be left alone to talk. For example, if you spend ten minutes or more talking together when your partner comes home or after dinner, then your children will become accustomed to taking themselves off in this time. Children may protest but if you know they have time when they can be with each of you then it does no harm at all for them to understand that you have adult business to discuss together.

When you don't agree

However well we felt we knew our partners before we had our children we will get to know a whole lot more about ourselves and about them as we each deal with the demands of

parenthood. One of the unpleasant shocks can be finding our partner doesn't get as involved as we would like or we don't see eye to eye over how we bring up our children.

If our partner doesn't get as involved as we want we have to look at the possible reasons:

- He hasn't got much time. Many men feel resentful that their working week demands so much of their time they cannot be with their children as often as they would wish. This can become a vicious circle. Because a man doesn't have time he cannot get to know his children and so feels lost and uncertain about how to react with them.

    This problem can be worked out by a couple together, depending on their circumstances. For example, if the working partner returns home late perhaps they could spend time with the children while the other one prepares supper to have later when the children are in bed.

- He feels uncomfortable with the children. A man who has little experience of children may feel inadequate and self-conscious. Unfortunately, some women can quite unconsciously make their partners feel inadequate. They are impatient with his inability to put on a nappy; they are critical that he excites the children just when they've calmed down for the evening. For the man, looking after his children becomes an increasingly unrewarding experience.

    When these situations arise then the mother can give her partner more confidence by tactfully demonstrating how to handle any difficulties. She can let him do things his own way and accept this is different to her way. Women sometimes have ambivalent feelings about sharing childcare. On the one hand they want the practical support, but emotionally they are reluctant to hand over control, or they feel anxious about being displaced.

Sharing discipline

Having children can often highlight differences in attitude between a couple. For instance, one may be easy going and laid back while the other likes things to be organised and clear cut.

One partner, for example, may have strong views that children should be encouraged to be organised and clear up after themselves. The other partner may feel this is unnecessary or can't be bothered to enforce rules and allows the children to leave their things lying around. Or, one parent may want to limit the amount of television their child watches while the other allows them to watch whatever they want.

In each of these instances, one parent feels they are being undermined by the other, while the second parent probably feels themselves under pressure from the first one. If a compromise cannot be worked out then these daily niggles become a constant source of irritation.

In addition, the couple's relationship with the child becomes weakened. One parent finds they are doing all the telling off and feels resentful that they always have to be Bad Guy. The other partner opts out of imposing discipline and becomes Nice Guy. When this happens the parents are unable to share the good and the bad bits about bringing up their children and their roles are split. Children are quick to detect and exploit rifts but even though they may use the situation to their advantage it gives the child too much power. It isn't in a child's best interest to manipulate adults.

Not in front of the children

Differences should always be worked out by the couple in private. Both partners may have to decide to give some ground. For example, the partner who insists on tidiness may agree to relax in some areas in exchange for being backed and supported by the other partner. Or

the parent who wants to limit their child's television viewing may allow a little more leeway in order that the other parent will feel comfortable about disciplining the child.

The most important job of all

Bringing another person into the world and helping them grow physically, mentally, emotionally and spiritually is one of the most important and rewarding jobs any of us can do. And yet looking after children has no tangible rewards. You can't look around at the end of the day and admire a tidy house or think of the money that's been earned from your labour. Quite the opposite, you may be only too conscious of the blobs of sticky finger paint all over the house and the money that's gone out of your purse rather than into it.

Despite the lip-service paid to the importance of parenting, in practice it often feels lonely and frustrating. Endless hours of tedious play, caring, tidying away, mopping up spilled drinks or tears produce no end product and no public accolades. But the other side of the coin is the joy and the selfless love which is different to any other relationship. When we share our child's pride at mastering some new skill, when we see the world fresh and new through their eyes or when their hugs communicate trust and love we know our life is much richer.

In bringing up our children we work with a short-term and a long-term perspective. There is the need to get through today, to enjoy the moment and to deal creatively with any problems. In the long-term we know our children are setting out on their journey of independence, heading towards the day when they live a life separate from us. Our children are on loan. We must enjoy them while we can and help them to become the best that they can be.